Contents

Hospitality:
Life in a Time of Fear

Finding Meaning and Purpose
In a Fearful World

Steve Clapp and Fred Bernhard

Cover by Custom Maid Design

A LifeQuest Publication

...d Purpose
...orld

Steve Clapp and Fred Bernhard

For further information, contact: LifeQuest, 6404 S. Calhoun Street, Fort Wayne, Indiana 46807; DadofTia@aol.com; 219-744-6510.

The authors of this book are not law enforcement professionals, terrorism authorities, home security experts, lawyers, physicians, meteorologists, or Internet gurus. This book is not intended as a resource for safe living but as a guide to a spiritually-based hospitality, which helps us live less fearfully.

The names and/or locations of some persons in the examples in this book have been changed to protect their privacy.

Biblical quotations, unless otherwise noted, are from the New Revised Standard Version of the Bible, copyrighted 1989 by the Division of Christian Education, National Council of Churches, and are used by permission.

ISBN 1-893270-08-4

Manufactured in the United States of America

This book is dedicated to:

Those killed in the tragic events of September 11, 2001.

Those who lost loved ones on September 11, 2001.

The police officers, fire fighters, emergency medical technicians, and military personnel who risk their lives to protect others.

The journalists, politicians, and business leaders of integrity who struggle with how to interpret and respond to the fears and issues of our time.

The silent victims of hunger in Afghanistan and around the world, including North America.

Postal employees and others who work today in more stressful conditions than in the past.

All people of faith who seek God's help in moving past their fears and reaching out to others.

We extend our thanks for the contributions made to this book by: Jan Fairchild, Debra Haffner, Kristen Leverton Helbert, Celia King, Claire Long, Randy Maid, Jerry Peterson, Sara Sprunger, and the staff of Evangel Press.

So we have known and believe the love that God has for us. God is love, and those who abide in love abide in God, and God abides in them. Love has been perfected among us in this: that we may have boldness on the day of judgment, because as he is, so are we in this world. There is no fear in love, but perfect love casts out fear; for fear has to do with punishment; and whoever fears has not reached perfection in love.

We love because he first loved us. Those who say, "I love God," and hate their brothers or sisters, are liars; for those who do not love a brother or sister whom they have seen, cannot love God whom they have not seen.

1 John 4:16-20

Introduction:
The Dark Day

September 11 had been a dark day for Steve Clapp since 1996 when his mother died on that date. He and his wife Sara knew the day would be even darker in 2001 because they were planning to attend the funeral service for a wonderful, bright, troubled young adult who had taken his own life. Chris had been married to their daughter until 1999. While the magnitude of his emotional problems proved fatal to that marriage, their daughter and the rest of the family had never stopped loving him. His suicide literally ripped a piece from their hearts.

Steve had gone to an early breakfast meeting with a friend to discuss some church business. When he left the restaurant, he noticed that the sun was out and the birds were singing; but that and the pleasant breakfast had done little to lift his spirits. As he drove to a Pak Mail outlet to ship a package, he started listening to National Public Radio's Morning Edition. Pulling into Pak Mail's parking lot, he heard the report of an airplane crashing into the Pentagon. He had been so preoccupied thinking about Chris and the funeral, that he thought perhaps he had misunderstood the broadcast. Surely that couldn't have happened.

The Pak Mail employees knew nothing about the Pentagon but were listening to news about a crash into one of the towers of the World Trade Center. Steve was shocked by the news and also reflected that he must have been very preoccupied to have thought he heard the Pentagon rather than the World Trade Center.

But of course it had been both the Pentagon and the World Trade Center. And that was only the start of the day's tragedy. By the end, there would be another crash into the remaining tower, the loss of United Airlines Flight 93 in western Pennsylvania, and the complete collapse of both towers. Police officers, fire fighters, and emergency medical technicians would risk and even lose their lives in efforts to save others.

Those events were followed by mounting anxiety about what other acts of terrorism were likely to happen. While that anxiety is not as high as this book goes to press as it was on September 11, 2001, it has not gone away. We fear further airline disasters, anthrax and smallpox infection, and other acts of terrorism. Further disasters could well have taken place between the writing of these words and your reading of them. We know that we are not safe.

For those of us in North America and for much of the world, the events of that day created a rupture in time. We are not the same individually or collectively as we were. We will remember for the rest of our lives what we were doing when we learned of those acts of terrorism.

Fred Bernhard is senior pastor of a church near Greenville, Ohio. He and his staff were having their regular Tuesday morning breakfast meeting at a restaurant. A waitress interrupted them to say, "A plane just flew into the World Trade Center." But the report seemed too strange to be true, and they continued with their meeting. Then she came to them again, saying that another plane flew into the other tower. "Come, look at the television for yourselves," she urged them, sensing their difficulty comprehending the news. Perplexed but still not convinced, they completed their agenda.

On the way out of the restaurant, they saw a replay on a television set; and the grim reality overwhelmed them. Their carefully made plans were pushed aside as they worked to stay on top of the developing news and to respond to the spiritual needs of the church and community. Like tens of thousands of churches around the country, they opened their sanctuary for prayer and scheduled a special service of worship.

Fred later apologized to the waitress for their insensitivity to her that morning. She understood and said, "I knew you heard me, but you couldn't grasp what I was telling you. Who could?"

The Fear Stays

Prior to the events of that day, many of us in North America seemed to be living in a wonderful age. The economy, although weaker than in the late 1990s, was strong; unemployment was low; and many people were enjoying a relatively high standard of living. Advances in medication and in medical procedures have increased the life expectancy and raised the quality of life for many. Computer technology and the continued development of the Internet have greatly improved our access to information and the speed of our communication with others.

But all was not well even then. Not really. Tens of thousands of people were dying each day from hunger and malnutrition–not only in countries like Afghanistan but also within the boundaries of North America. Lives were being lost to accidental firearm discharges, alcoholism, tobacco, AIDS, drunk driving, abortion, and suicide. Lives of young men and women were being forever changed through unwanted pregnancies. Companies and individuals indulged in acts of disregard for the environment–giving little thought to the air, water, land, or animals. None of these concerns forced their way into our consciousness, into the priorities of politicians, or onto the front pages of the news media like the events of September 11, 2001. The issues, however, were there. And still are.

The aftermath of September 11 is still very fresh, and some people will live with the tragedy for the rest of their lives.

- Many families lost loved ones in the events of September 11. They go on with their lives, but violence has left a mark that they cannot forget. In the *New York Times Magazine* for November 11, 2001, Lisa Belkin writes about "Life without Father," describing the experiences of two families trying to rebuild after deaths in the World Trade Center. The mothers are working hard to help their children grow without hatred and fear, but that is a difficult job. One mother asks, "When the unthinkable happens to a child, how do you tell him the world is safe?" [p. 114]

- A survivor of the World Trade Center tragedy now works in a building filled with posters of persons listed as "missing." She knows many of those people, and her heart breaks as she walks the gauntlet of the posters. The rush down the stairs of the tower on that Tuesday morning is so hard-wired into the neurons of her brain that the sight of a stairway fills her with panic. She wonders if life can ever be "normal" again.

- One couple, whose son is among the missing from the World Trade Center collapse, left their New England home and moved to New York for two months immediately after the tragedy. They walked the streets and went to the hospitals with pictures of their son. They searched all the boroughs of New York, thinking he might have been dazed and starting wandering, not knowing where he was. Their daughter dropped out of college to be with them, not so much because she believed that her brother could be found as because she wanted to give her parents emotional support in what she knew was a futile search. At the start of the third month, they reluctantly went home.

- A family living in an apartment near the World Trade Center was forced to move. Debris from the Center had so filled their apartment that they had to throw away clothing, books, a computer, and, most painfully of all, the stuffed toys of their son. They are thankful not to have lost anyone in the September 11 attack, but they feel their home has been stolen from them. They are debating whether to stay in New York or to move to another part of the country.

- A business owner in the area of the World Trade Center used his own assets to keep paying employees, even though sales were off by 68% the first two months after the attack. He feels torn between the desire to stay in the same location and the reality that his store may never return to its sales volume before the attack.

- A man in northern Indiana died because a heart that was to be transplanted in him had to be redirected when the airplanes were grounded on September 11. The heart saved the life of another person, but that is little consolation to his family.

- A military officer who worked in the Pentagon and lost three close friends in the September 11 crash has asked for reassignment because the daily reminders of their presence are too painful.

- A woman who worked in the World Trade Center escaped from one of the towers only seconds before its collapse.

Now she is filled with grief for her friends who died and with guilt over the fact that she survived. She knows the guilt is irrational, but it continues. Those who died fill her dreams each night, and her days are still walking nightmares.

The fear and grief, of course, are not limited to those who were directly connected to people who died in New York, Washington, or Pennsylvania. We are far more connected to one another than we ordinarily realize. In the 1960s, a psychologist named Stanley Milgram gave 160 people in Oklahoma a packet with the name and address of a stockbroker who lived in Massachusetts. He asked them to pass or send the packet to a person they knew who could get it closer to the broker. Each person in the chain was to continue the process. Most of the packets reached the person in only five or six steps. That experiment is the basis for the phrase "six degrees of separation."

Both of us have really experienced the truth of that concept as we've visited with people around North America about what happened on September 11, 2001. The number of people related to someone who died in those attacks or a friend of someone who died is enormous. And then there are all the people who know someone else who knew someone who died. It often seems like two or three degrees of separation rather than six.

When news of the World Trade Center attack first came to Steve Clapp, he was immediately concerned about his cousin, who lives and works in Manhattan. He remembered being able to see the towers from her apartment window. Was she all right? Could her work have taken her into the towers that day? He tried calling repeatedly, but of course the circuits were busy and calls could not go through. Fortunately his cousin knew that he would be concerned and sent him an e-mail from her place of work. Millions of people in North America suffered similar anxiety. And anxiety continues:

- A man in his seventies, trying to fly out of Eugene, Oregon, was upset by airport security there, who wanded him, patted him down, made him take his shoes off and send them through the x-ray machine, and went through every single item in his carry-on. Then when he reached the gate, shaking from what was for him a very unpleasant ordeal, he found himself singled out for another wanding, pat down, and carry-on search. By the time he was on the plane, he felt that he had been a victim of terrorism himself.

- A postal employee is considering early retirement because of the anxiety of handling so much mail each day. She does not feel reassured by the official statements about anthrax and other biological weapons. She takes medication for anxiety but still has difficulty sleeping at night.

- A Planned Parenthood employee is ready for a career change. Threats are nothing new in her work, but now a small amount of baby powder in an envelope is sufficient to set off an anthrax scare.

- A movie actress established a "safe house" in a western state and purchased gas masks for her five dogs! It's hard to conceive of her being the direct target of terrorist acts, but the fear is real to her and has changed her life.

- A woman who travels throughout North America and Europe fulfilling her sales responsibilities is looking for other work. She takes Valium before going to the airport but still feels overwhelmed by anxiety about flying.

- A single mother has had to arrange new child care. The child care center she had used for two years now keeps a gun on the premises–thinking that will reassure people. But this mother feels the presence of the gun is a greater danger than any terrorist.

Similar Title–Different Book

This is the third book on which we have collaborated. The first, *Widening the Welcome of Your Church*, was written for pastors and congregation members to help them practice the kind of biblical hospitality which helps a church grow. When people visit a church for the first time, the primary question on their minds usually is: "Is this a friendly church?" There are some people who seek anonymity in their initial worship experiences, but most people come to church in part because they want to be connected to others. If church members appear indifferent or too involved in their conversations with each other to reach out to visitors, then first timers are unlikely to become second timers. Response to *Widening the Welcome of Your Church* was enthusiastic, and the fourth printing of it was completed this summer.

Just a year ago a second joint book of ours was released: *Hospitality: Life without Fear.* In the workshops we conducted around North America, we increasingly became aware that many people were viewing "hospitality" as another program in the life of the church rather than as a way of life. We were also becoming increasingly aware that many people go through life filled with fear.

The news media and politicians have done a good job, both before and after September 11, 2001, keeping us informed about crime, illness, and threats to our personal safety. In fact there are ways in which they have done too good a job–causing people to feel almost immobilized by fear. Many of us are not comfortable around strangers, and some of us aren't sure how far to trust our friends and work colleagues. Our time is often called the Information Age, and that is a reasonable description. Some of that information, however, has made us painfully aware of the worst of which human beings are capable. It is an Age of Fear as well as of information.

We wrote *Hospitality: Life without Fear* to speak to the fears that often prevent people from connecting with each other and to show that hospitality isn't primarily a program for churches, synagogues, and mosques but a way of living that affects all relationships including family, friends, coworkers, neighbors, acquaintances, other drivers on the road, and clerks in stores. We wrote the book not primarily for congregations but for individuals who are seeking more meaningful lives.

But that book, while acknowledging the prevalence of fear in North America, was based on what has become an unrealistic assumption: that it is possible to develop a life without fear, or at least with very little fear. While the words from 1 John which appear opposite the first page of this introduction promise that "perfect love casts out fear," most of us have not reached a state of perfect love. And the events of September 11, 2001 have made fear a part of daily life for people around North America and have deepened the fears of people living in other parts of the world. We are not anytime soon going to experience *life without fear*, but we can find meaningful ways to deal with our fears and get on with our lives–we can live full lives even in *a time of fear*. And we are convinced one of the best roads to a meaningful life is to be found through the practice of hospitality which is part of a healthy spiritual life.

We are not experts on biological weapons, airplane travel, or terrorism. We have, however, focused much of our respective ministries on helping people develop meaningful hospitality; and the research organization which Steve Clapp directs has done significant research on the impact of hospitality–not just on congregations but on individuals. Hospitality, which grows out of a strong spiritual life, can provide the means to move forward in positive ways even in a time of great fear.

The Stone Wall

Steve Clapp and his wife Sara had become increasingly aware of the problems with a low stone wall which ran along the west side of their house. The wall was about three feet high and was constructed many decades ago out of dirt, timber, and some stone. Over the years, the timber had rotted, the dirt had been washed away, and both the wall and the long flower bed it supported had begun to slowly slide into their neighbor's yard. They knew that it would be an enormous task to dig out the old wall, get rid of all the rotting timbers, and build a new stone wall. They needed a motivational starting point, so they had two tons of new stone delivered to their home shortly before Labor Day weekend of 2001. And they pledged that they would start the project together that weekend.

Their goals for the weekend, however, were somewhat different. Steve thought that they would work an hour or perhaps two hours a day and make a good beginning on getting the old timbers and stone pulled out. Sara, always more ambitious and energetic, thought that labor was a very fitting way to celebrate Labor Day weekend! She didn't think they would get the project finished but did hope they would get the old wall out and perhaps complete a third of the new wall. Vision and drive can accomplish a lot. For Steve there was also a little guilt because he had not helped Sara much with the previous summer's work on a wall on the south side of their house.

The result was that they completed the entire wall that three-day weekend. They amazed themselves. The wall runs along a side of the house where few people see it, but Steve and Sara know it's there. And they know it will last. . . longer than they will live in the house. It will not slide; it will not slip. The stones which they recycled from the old wall and the new stones are heavy and solid. There are stones beneath the level of the soil that can't be seen and provide a very strong foundation.

But it is not a foundation that could have survived what happened at the World Trade Center. Steve Clapp had eaten on three occasions at the Windows on the World restaurant at the top of one of the World Trade Center towers. He was impressed each time with the sturdiness of the building. One of the meals was during an evening thunderstorm. The view was spectacular, and he felt quite safe. But of course the safety was to some extent an illusion. No building material that we have on this planet could have survived what happened at the Pentagon and the World Trade Center on Tuesday, September 11, 2001.

So we are shaken, and we are fearful in a way that we were not before that date. We do not feel safe. We do not know how to understand or deal with foes like this, with people whose intense zeal and fanaticism have them willing to sacrifice their own lives in order to kill others. Those of us in the United States know that the view of our country by other nations is very different than the way we see ourselves, but it is still difficult for most of us to understand the raw hatred of Osama bin Laden and others. And we wonder: how could this have happened, how can we be safe, and what can we count on in such a world?

The Old Testament Book of Ecclesiastes has been considered pessimistic by many people. Verses 1–8 of the third chapter describe the cycles of life:

> *For everything there is a season, and a time for*
> *every matter under heaven;*
> *a time to be born, and a time to die;*
> *a time to plant, and a time to*
> *pluck up what is planted;*
> *a time to kill, and a time to heal;*

> a time to break down, and a time to build up;
> a time to weep, and a time to laugh;
> a time to mourn, and a time to dance;
> a time to throw away stones,
>   and a time to gather stones together;
> a time to embrace, and a time
>   to refrain from embracing;
> a time to seek, and a time to lose;
> a time to keep, and a time to throw away;
> a time to tear, and a time to sew;
> a time to keep silence, and a time to speak;
> a time to love, and a time to hate;
> a time for war, and a time for peace.

At one level, the words are pessimistic, but they describe life as it is. There is a time to weep and a time to laugh. There is a time to keep silence and a time to speak. And tragically, throughout history, there have been times both of war and of peace.

We all live with the tragedy of what happened in New York, in Washington, and in the skies over Pennsylvania. And in the midst of that national, indeed global, tragedy, individuals are also carrying heavy personal loads with surgery, illness, grief, economic anxieties, and family problems bearing down on them. It takes considerable courage to deal with the challenges that come to tens of millions of people in North America every single day.

But the events of September 11 are also chronologically bookended by joy. Weddings were performed, children were born, and incredible acts of generosity took place both before and after September 11. The times to weep and to laugh can come in incredible proximity to each other. The bad news is that we are not safe from tragedy, and nothing can make us safe. Even giving up a tremendous number of our freedoms will not make us safe. But we can build solid foundations, like the house on the rock described in the Sermon on the Mount [Matthew 7:24–27]:

> *Everyone then who hears these words of mine*
> *and acts on them will be like a wise man who*
> *built his house on rock. The rain fell, the floods*
> *came, and the winds blew and beat on that*
> *house, but it did not fall, because it had been*
> *founded on rock. And everyone who hears these*

> *words of mine and does not act on them will be*
> *like a foolish man who built his house on sand.*
> *The rain fell, and the floods came and the winds*
> *blew and beat against that house, and it fell—*
> *and great was its fall!*

Unlike the World Trade Center, our spiritual houses need not collapse in difficult times if they are truly resting on the rock which is Christ. . . . And we built that house, our Lord tells us, by hearing His words and acting on them. We can provide the same kind of spiritual foundation for our lives that Steve and Sara provided in stone for the wall along the side of their house. It is work to build such a foundation, and it at times will strain our resources and energy. But once that foundation is built, we can withstand whatever life brings. Our Lord guides us in building that foundation.

What can we count on? Three things. Three very basic concepts that most of us learned when very young, but they remain true in all circumstances, for people of all ages.

First, we can count on the fact that God loves us and is with us no matter what happens. The universe is not entirely safe. Freedom is at the heart of creation, both for the natural world and for humanity as well. Some tragedy comes, some evil comes, and that evil even took the life of God's son on the cross. But God's love is a constant in the face of tragedy and evil. Just as the fire fighters, emergency medical technicians, police officers, and others sort through the rubble of the World Trade Center, God reaches out to us through the rubble of our lives with a love that never stops. And God continues to love us beyond this life.

We may not find all the bodies of those who were killed; but make no mistake about it, God has already found and claimed the lives of those people. Those who have died are in the comfort and love of God, unless they themselves have chosen to reject it. The promise of eternal life and of God's love existing without end is central to our faith; it is at the very heart of Christianity.

Second, we can count on experiencing God's grace through the compassion and the courage of other people. What happened in New York, in Washington, D.C., and in the skies of Pennsylvania shows both the worst and the best of which people are capable. And while people will at times let us down, we would do well to remember that most of God's love is conveyed to us through one another. We have seen considerable evidence of that following September 11:

- Think about the fire fighters and police who went charging into the buildings to save others, risking and even losing their own lives.

- Think about the fire fighters, the police, and the construction worker volunteers who continued to sort through the debris in New York City, working in dangerous conditions in the hope of saving others.

- Think about the people on United Airlines Flight 93 who calmly and with little hesitation told their loved ones on the phone that they were going to do something about the hijacking. We will never know exactly what happened on that plane, but we know it slammed into a field in western Pennsylvania rather than becoming another weapon against another target.

- Think about a woman in her seventies in Bloomington, Indiana, who heard a group of young males talking about their plans to find and punish "some Arabs." She walked right up to them, told them they should be ashamed of themselves, and they disbursed.

Third, we can count on the fact that God, ultimately, will have the last word. Consider the impact of two books. One of them was by Adolph Hitler and provided the philosophical foundation for the Third Reich. The book, which Hitler dictated to a colleague, was titled *Mein Kampf*, meaning "My Struggle" or "My Battle." Reading the book and transcripts of Hitler's speeches has been a requirement in some seminary classes because faculty want students to be aware of the ways in which Hitler had used the language of the Bible and the traditions of the Christian faith to justify hatred toward Jewish people. Hitler indeed distorted the Christian faith in ways very similar to those in which Osama bin Laden and others have distorted the Islamic faith.

The second book was not written for publication. It was the personal diary of an adolescent girl named Anne Frank, who recorded her thoughts during the period in which she and her family hid from the Nazi powers in an annex of rooms above her father's office in Amsterdam. She was later arrested and died of typhus at the concentration camp Bergen-Belsen. Living in constant fear, she spoke in the diary about her overall faith in the goodness of people.

Hitler appeared to triumph over Anne Frank. She was one of the many stamped out by his tyranny. But now, decades later, Hitler is gone–and Hitler's book and speeches are studied by few people except historians and seminary students. But *The Diary of Anne Frank* has been translated into sixty-seven languages and has sold millions and millions of copies. It is one of the most popular books ever published. God has the last word. The quiet goodness of the Anne Franks of the world ultimately counts for more than the power and sickness of the Hitlers. And though it may not appear that God is in control, the victories of evil are never permanent.

The floods will come. We will all encounter times of suffering, and we will either become better or worse through those times. But when the foundation of our lives is in the rock of God's word, we can face the future with confidence, knowing that in this life and in the life to come, God always has the last word.

A Different Way

Many of our fears, particularly those concerning strangers and our safety, have the ability to paralyze us from meaningful relationships. The truth is that many of us do not know how to relate comfortably to strangers; and we sometimes do not know how to relate comfortably to our spouses, children, parents, friends, and coworkers.

We are writing this book because we are convinced that there is a different way of living–one which closes the distance between ourselves and other people. That way of living is impossible unless our lives are rooted in God. We are convinced that God is calling all of us to lives of true biblical hospitality, that we need to increasingly view those around us as gifts from God and to recognize the presence of Christ in others, including those we may at first be tempted to dislike or even disown.

Henri Nouwen, in his classic book *Reaching Out*, said this about the world in which we live:

> In our world full of strangers, estranged from their
> past, culture and country, from their neighbors,
> friends, and family, from their deepest self and
> their God, we witness a painful search for a
> hospitable place where life can be lived without
> fear and where community can be found [p. 46].

Our lives do not have to be filled with fear. While there are dangerous elements in the world, all of us were created out of the love of God; and creation is fundamentally good. For us, hospitality can be defined in this way:

Hospitality involves recognizing the presence of
Christ in family, friends, coworkers, neighbors,
and complete strangers. It means responding to
others as we would respond to the presence of
Christ in our midst.

There are no insignificant relationships. Every single person we encounter, even if only in a passing phone conversation, is a child of God–and Christ is present in that person. We affect one another in far deeper ways than we realize, and we are continually given opportunities to learn from others about the world which we share and about our own lives.

One of the major themes of this book is that blessings flow to us as we recognize the presence of Christ in others and reach out to one another. A life grounded in hospitality, a life which seeks to recognize the presence of Christ in each person we encounter, is not always going to be an easy life. It is often easier to be driven by our fears and to stay removed from others. But that kind of life is not the one to which God has called us.

Hospitality, of course, is not always safe. There's a small chance that someone we choose to befriend will turn out to be manipulative or dishonest. We may occasionally extend hospitality toward those who reject us. We may find that the practice of hospitality leads us into contact with persons we would otherwise have avoided. But the potential for blessings from a life centered in hospitality is much greater than the risks which are involved. If we take our relationships with God seriously, hospitality is not an optional way of living. When we fail to recognize the presence of Christ in others, we are in fact cutting ourselves off from the blessings God wishes to give us.

Steve and Fred

Tips from the United States Postal Service

What should make me suspect a piece of mail?
- It's unexpected or from someone you don't know.
- It's addressed to someone no longer at your address.
- It's handwritten and has no return address or bears one that you can't confirm is legitimate.
- It's lopsided or lumpy in appearance.
- It's sealed with excessive amounts of tape.
- It's marked with restrictive endorsements such as "Personal" or "Confidential."

What should I do with a suspicious piece of mail?
- Don't handle a letter or package that you suspect is contaminated.
- Don't shake it, bump it, or sniff it.
- Wash your hands thoroughly with soap and water.
- Notify local law enforcement authorities.

Chapter One:
Fear Serves a Purpose

Concept: Some of our fears are healthy and can protect us as individuals and communities from the very real dangers of our world. We need to be aware, however, that widespread fear also serves a slightly different purpose for politicians, journalists, and some businesses.

On September 11 and the days immediately following, most of us in North America were glued to our television sets. New facts kept emerging, and the drama of the unfolding events bound us together in a kind of unity. Both of the authors of this book were impressed by the quality of most of the reporting. Newscasters like Peter Jennings, Diane Sawyer, and Charlie Gibson displayed not only their professionalism but also their humanity as they did not try to cover their personal pain and horror over the events which transpired. We name those three simply because they were the ones we saw most frequently, but our sense is that high standards prevailed in all the media.

But as the days went by, many of us began to feel that the hypnotism of the media, particularly that of television, trapped us and made it more difficult to move on with our lives. Although there were less significant events to report, the television coverage still dominated our days. On one talk show, a guest shared the obvious: "Watching too much of the coverage on television is bad for small children." And a member of the audience said, "It's bad for all of us."

What is the line between staying informed and becoming obsessed in a way that is harmful to one's life? What is the line between professional reporting and needlessly focusing on the frightening and the terrible for the sake of ratings? Those are not particularly easy questions to answer. A cartoon in the November 12, 2001, *Newsweek* shows a jet fighter with a military pilot in the front seat and a yelling passenger in the back seat.

The passenger is labeled "Media" and is screaming: "Are we there yet? Are we there yet?"

Fear serves a significant number of purposes in our world. Healthy fear certainly protects us from danger, and only the foolish ignore such concerns. Fear also:

- gives power to politicians who promise to protect us.
  The fear following the events of September 11, 2001
  has prompted a willingness of the American public
  to give up rights and convenience to the government
  in exchange for the promise of safety.

- gives power to news media who receive higher ratings
  and more advertising dollars when fear prompts higher
  readership and viewership.

- gives power to those businesses and industries which
  offer insurance and security services. And to those
  companies who have learned how to use patriotism
  as a marketing device.

We do not mean to imply that the motivations of these persons and groups are sinister or evil. The reality is, however, that fear causes us to respond differently; and there are always those who gain from high levels of fear in society. That was true even before the events of September 11.

If It Bleeds, It Leads

"If it bleeds, it leads" is an old journalism guideline; but it has tremendous impact on radio, television, and Internet reporting as well as on newspapers and magazines. While the violent crime rate in the United States has decreased in recent years, reporting of crime continues to increase. According to one study by the Center for Media and Public Affairs, the television coverage of murder increased by 336% between 1995 and 2000. Statistics from some major cities (Boston, Chicago, Houston, Los Angeles, Phoenix, and Pittsburgh) near the end of 2001 suggest that homicide rates may be going up again but not at a rate approaching the increase in news coverage.

Following the tragedy at Columbine High School in Littleton, Colorado, juvenile crime has come under very close scrutiny by the news media. Actions which would have received almost no publicity twenty years ago now become the subject of national headlines. Barry Glassner, a sociology professor and author of *The Culture of Fear*, says, "The images of young people running from Columbine have been shown hundreds of times. I don't mean to minimize the seriousness of the incident, but it gives the impression it's still with us, and that these kinds of events happen more often than they do" [Quoted in *The Desert Sun*, October 17, 1999].

News media reporting on both natural and human tragedy keeps some of us in perpetual fear of flying, driving, or sharing in social gatherings–including school. The news media, of course, are only part of the problem. Many played on our fears prior to the events of September 11, 2001:

- Politicians want us to be afraid of crime and to have confidence that their "get tough" policies will keep us safe. Most of us, in our more rational moments, have learned not to believe everything we hear from politicians; but the emphasis they place on crime, as an election issue and as a continuing budget issue, affects all of us.

- Many television dramas and motion pictures feed our fears. We may find a certain measure of enjoyment in the charge of adrenalin that comes from fear during a show, but the memory of the fear often stays with us and affects our view of the world–even though we are not likely to face the evils that Mel Gibson, Sarah Michelle Gellar, Denzel Washington, and Sigourney Weaver do on the screen.

- Social service organizations sometimes appeal to our fears of drugs and violence in the process of raising money for their good work. Some of the best fund-raising appeals for organizations that work directly with children remind us of the dangers in our society.

- Ministers, including (we are embarrassed to confess) the authors of this book, talk about the dangers in our society as we call people to greater reliance on

God. The call to lives more centered on God is an appropriate message for every age, but we sometimes foster an "us" (in the church) versus "them" (in the world) way of looking at life.

- Some clergy and religious groups have appealed to the rampant fear of homosexuality in our society to build financial and political support for measures that fail to acknowledge the human rights of persons of homosexual orientation. The fear of homosexuality which has been engendered in some heterosexuals is both irrational and destructive.

- Real estate agents, builders, and security system companies may emphasize neighborhood crime rates, the possibility of burglary, and the need for home security as they sell houses and services. Some people now live in apartment buildings and housing complexes which give the appearance of being fortresses, designed to keep the occupants safe from danger.

And of course there are many other kinds of fear which affect us. We fear the illness or death of our loved ones; we fear our own illness or death; we fear financial catastrophe; we fear letting down the people who count on us; and we fear that we are not making the most of the opportunities God has given us.

As we have already pointed out, not all fears are bad or harmful. Fear of fires, tornadoes, hurricanes, and earthquakes helps people exercise caution which saves lives. Fear of illness motivates us to seek medical care and to make lifestyle improvements. Psalm 111:10 reminds us that: "The fear of the LORD is the beginning of wisdom; all those who practice it have a good understanding." There are many of us who might do well to cultivate a healthy fear of God, particularly in terms of obedience.

We Are Changed

All of those things were true before planes crashed into the World Trade Center, the Pentagon, and a field in western Pennsylvania. They were true before mail carried the threat of anthrax. We also wonder what events are yet to unfold. Our book *Hospitality: Life without Fear* had a relatively short life; we asked the publisher to pull it after less than a year because we wanted to replace it with the book you are reading now. But books for the most part have relatively long lives. They can easily remain on the shelves of traditional bookstores, in catalogs, and in Internet bookstores for five to ten years after they are published; and they can remain on the shelves of individuals and libraries for decades. Some books, which are truly classics, far outlive their authors.

We don't know that this book will outlive its authors. Both of us hope for long life! But we do wonder what events of terrorism and of response to terrorism are yet to emerge. As a people in North America, we may be feeling considerably better or considerably worse as you read these words than at the time they are being written. What seems clear is that, no matter what the future brings, our view of life has been transformed:

- In an America Online poll reported on September 25, 2001, people were asked what had changed the most for them since that attacks. Forty percent of those responding said that they had a new sense of patriotism, but 26% said that they primarily felt scared and uneasy. Three-fourths of the respondents felt that the changes would be permanent.

- On September 21, 2001, Susan Forste, a computer designer at Amnesty International in New York City, wrote these words to family in Indiana: "You see the hole in the skyline. Everyone is stunned, and the disaster is the only topic of conversation. Everywhere there are posters of the missing and votive candles. It was so, so sad when they started appearing. Two blocks away from me is a firehouse with seven men missing. Flowers and candles have turned it into a shrine, and local businesses have set up a fund to help the men's families [Squad 18 Family Fund]." The hole in the skyline, and the holes in the hearts of people remain with us–and will still be with us even when the last of the posters come down and the candles disappear.

- Several estimates have been made on the increases in prescriptions for anti-anxiety drugs in the last

two weeks in September. The estimates range from
8.6% to 68%.

- The October 22, 2001, issue of *Time* reported a 100%
  increase in applications for concealed weapons in
  the state of Texas since September 11.

- The same issue of *Time* reported that 67% of those
  reached in a telephone poll felt it likely that there
  would be a terrorist attack in the U.S. in the coming
  twelve months at a major public event, and 64%
  felt there would be an attack on the water supply.

- *Newsweek* reported in their November 12, 2001,
  issue that 68% of young adults in the country
  believe that the terror attacks have made those
  their age more serious about study and work.

- A Christian Community study of members of
  Christian congregations, in early November of 2001,
  reported that 89% felt significantly more fearful
  about their personal safety than they had before
  the terrorist attacks.

Certainly the polls and statistics from 2002 and 2003 will
show some differences from what we are highlighting here, but
the impact of the attacks will still be with us–even if nothing
further happens. The attacks have also caused significant
changes in how we view the news and in the access the news
media have to information.

The Pew Research Center found that right after the attacks,
65% of persons thirty years of age and younger in the United
States were following the stories "very closely." That percentage
was lower than for other age groups. But by just the middle of
October, that percentage rose to 78%, which was essentially the
same as for older age groups. [Reported by Martha Irvine in an
Associated Press article on November 13, 2001]

Access to information, however, is of critical importance if
the news we receive is to be accurate and helpful. As in past
times of conflict, the United States government is well aware
that it is fighting a public relations campaign as it seeks support
for new regulations and for military actions in response to the

terrorist attacks. The *New York Times* on November 11, 2001, reminds us that control of information has caused some allies to feel uncomfortable:

> *If the United States has a public relations problem among its allies, it boils down to this: many Europeans feel they have precious little information they can trust. They rely on conflicting and equally unverifiable claims from Pentagon briefings and Taliban news conferences, and are increasingly unwilling to believe either side.*

Secretary of Defense Donald Rumsfeld refused to allow a reporter from the Associated Press to go with him on an overseas trip which permitted representatives of the TV networks, the *L.A. Times*, *USA Today*, the *Wall Street Journal*, and the *Washington Post*. Yet the Associated Press is the major and sometimes only source of national and international news to many newspapers and broadcast outlets. An editorial in the November 13, 2001, issue of the *Journal Gazette* warns:

> *Rumsfeld's decision is part of a frightening pattern by the Bush administration to close off independent sources of news in the war on terrorism. With TV networks succumbing to pressure from the Bush administration to heavily edit any video of Osama bin Laden, Arab nations with access to the Al Jazeera satellite channel are receiving a more complete picture of some events than Americans.*

It's not our intention to vilify those in government who are exercising control over access to information. From an historical perspective, similar controls have been attempted during past military conflicts. The government obviously has a vested interest in nurturing patriotism and protecting information which could be harmful to troops in combat. It's important for us, however, not to uncritically accept all that we are told. As this book goes to press, there are some questions which we have not heard the news media ask with much force. We hope that, by the time you read these words, answers are available:

- Are civilian deaths in Afghanistan accurately reported?

- Are we being told the truth about the readiness of the government to handle bioterrorism?

- Are we being made more fearful of bioterrorism than the facts actually warrant? Does the average person have as much to fear as many in the government and in the news media cause us to think? October and November of 2001 brought repeated news stories about anthrax. Was the public being properly warned or being made needlessly fearful?

- Was it really necessary for the U. S. government to detain hundreds or even thousands of young men of Arab descent following September 11, 2001? Why were there such long delays in the release of many of them?

- Are the increasingly invasive and cumbersome policies at airports really making flights safer, or are they primarily public relations ploys with little practical consequence except delays? How much of the problem is in the security procedures, and how much is actually in the persons responsible for those procedures?

We do not mean to imply that questions like these are always easy to answer. We also do not mean to imply that the government and the news media are deliberately misleading us in each instance. Some politicians and journalists are asking those important questions, but more should be.

In many ways, the people of the United States grew closer together following the terrorist attacks and experienced a renewed sense of healthy patriotism. We not only affirm the value of those transformations but also pray that our bonds with one another can be deepened even more in the months and the years ahead. The September 11 events made us rethink what is important in life, and many of us have begun to take our faith more seriously since that date. That does not, however, mean that we should uncritically accept everything that we are told by politicians, media, and businesses. We need to think carefully and critically about what has happened and about what the future brings.

The Need to Move Ahead

We mourn those who have died. We are concerned about fire fighters, police officers, military, and others who risk their well-being to protect us. We are, as a people, taking more medication and experiencing significantly greater anxiety than before the terrorist attacks. How do we move ahead with our lives?

1. We need to carefully assess the information we receive and be careful not to overreact. Some of us need to watch less television. Hearing the same warnings over and over can immobilize us. The two of us do not claim to be experts on terrorism, but we do have some observations to share:

- Unless we propose to hide in the wilderness for the next decade, there is no way to be fully safe. Most of us, fortunately, are not as individuals on the "hit list" of any terrorist. Should we be affected, it will be because we are at the wrong place at the wrong time.

- While there are significant inconveniences in the screening process today for air travel, the truth still is that most of us are safer flying that driving our own automobiles.

- Most of us as individuals are highly unlikely to receive anthrax or any other dangerous substance in our mail. If you do find a powdery substance in the mail, leave the room, wash your hands (to keep anthrax spores from going to your lungs), and call 911. Anthrax can be treated. [*People*, October 29, 2001, p. 103]

- We should control access to television and the Internet for children. Young children respond to news like the World Trade Center tragedy with immediate concern for themselves and those they love. "Will a plane fly into our house?" Repeated news stories will cause repeated anxiety for young children. Older children need information, but they also need to have their parents talk with them about what they are experiencing. Parents need to be careful not to pass their own anxiety along to their children.

- We need to be careful not to overreact to rumors that we hear at work, in the neighborhood, over the Internet, or through traditional news media. Don't automatically assume the worst. Find out the facts.

- Healthy patriotism is valuable. It connects us to one
  another and makes us appreciative of the blessings
  we collectively receive. Those of us fortunate enough
  to be in the United States or Canada have a great
  deal for which to be thankful. We should be careful,
  however, that patriotism does not cause us to hate
  those from other countries. One newspaper reader in
  Fort Wayne, Indiana, wrote to express his anger over
  pictures of Afghan children appearing in the paper.
  "It was the parents of those children who have allowed
  the leaders of their country to protect the people who
  attack thousands of innocent Americans. Stop using
  your newspaper to try to stimulate sympathy for a
  people who have no morals or decency." That kind
  of hatred is based on ignorance–ignorance of the reality
  that the Afghan people have also been victims of the
  Taliban and of Osama bin Laden.

**2. We need to place emphasis on the development of
the spiritual life, including a healthy hospitality.** Our faith
in God provides the strength which we need to move ahead with
our lives. Paul expressed it well in his Letter to the Philippians:

> *Forgetting what lies behind and straining forward
> to what lies ahead, I press on toward the goal for
> the prize of the heavenly call of God in Christ Jesus*
> [3:13b-14].

Paul uses athletic imagery, straining forward for the prize in a
race, to communicate a powerful message about the Christian
life. We are challenged not to be trapped by the events of the
past but to move into the future with confidence. We should
begin each day with confidence that, no matter what happens,
God will be with us and with those we love.

We are not necessarily promised that we will always be
spared tragedy in our lives. In fact Christ's earthly life ended
painfully on a cross. But suffering is never the last word.

We do not know the precise means through which God
works in our lives. We do not know why certain people died in
the Pentagon and the World Trade Center catastrophes and
other people, in sometimes miraculous ways, were spared. It
does seem a sign of God's grace and protection that the final

death counts were not as high as they might have been—especially considering the reality that as many as 50,000 people have been in the World Trade Center on some days and as many as 23,000 in the Pentagon. One survivor shared this view shortly after the September 11 tragedy:

> *I do not understand why I was able to get out alive when so many of my friends are missing—probably dead. . . . But I know I am going to live differently from this moment on. I was spared, and I want to show that I was spared for something worthwhile. I've already wasted too much of the life God gave me. There are too many times I should have been more forgiving, more loving, more accepting, more ready to do the right thing. Why does it take disaster for us to examine our lives and start living as we should?*
> [Personal e-mail from a September 11 survivor]

We get on with our lives, confident that God protects us as fully as possible consistent with the natural laws of the universe, but more than that we remain confident that God is with us no matter what happens. Paul's letters carry a recurring theme that nothing separates us from the love of Christ. In Romans, he writes:

> *For I am convinced that neither death, nor life, nor angels, nor rulers, nor things present, nor things to come, nor powers, nor height, nor depth, nor anything else in all creation, will be able to separate us from the love of God in Christ Jesus our Lord*
> [8:38-39].

And the love of Christ is made real in our relationships with others. Hospitality brings us closer to others and closer to Christ.

Anthrax and Other Biological Weapons

- You can contract anthrax through inhaling the spores, eating food contaminated with it, or coming into contact with it through an open wound.

- Anthrax spores, when not actively infecting organisms, can go into a hibernation and can last up to eighty years in the soil.

- Anthrax itself is not highly contagious. The strains of anthrax known as of the date of this writing can only be contracted through direct contact with spores. Those with the disease do not exhale spores.

- During the 1980s, a religious cult in Oregon caused illness in hundreds of people through a bioterrorism attack of *Salmonella typhimurium.* The attack was downplayed by the government, in part out of fear of causing copy-cat crimes.

- In the 1950s, government scientists in the United States conducted tests to explore how Soviet cities could be attacked with anthrax germs. Noninfectious aerosols were released in Saint Louis, Minneapolis, and Winnipeg. Those cities were chosen because of climates and sizes similar to potential Soviet targets.

- The United States and the Soviet Union took over a decade in the 1950s and 1960s to learn the key secrets of biological warfare. Iraq, however, learned to make thousands of gallons of anthrax and botulinum in only two or three years. The availability of information truly makes germs "the poor man's atom bomb."

*Based on information in **Germs–Biological Weapons and America's Secret War** by Judith Miller, Stephen Engelberg, and William Broad [Simon and Schuster, 2001] and the October 22, 2001 issue of **Time Magazine**.*

Chapter Two:
Fear, Loneliness, and Hospitality

> **Concept:** We live in a fearful time and have learned to lock our cars, homes, hearts, and minds. God offers us the courage to reach out to others and to keep fear from overwhelming our lives.

At one o'clock in the morning, Steve went to a 24-hour drugstore to get an allergy prescription refilled. He had forgotten to do it earlier in the day and knew he would need it before conducting a workshop that started at eight o'clock the next morning. A workshop leader with a drippy nose does not inspire confidence!

A woman named Mable, in her late seventies, was the only other customer at the prescription counter. She and Steve had a brief conversation in which he learned that she also had forgotten to get a prescription refilled earlier in the day, but hers was for high blood pressure. After she left, the pharmacist quickly took care of Steve's prescription.

When Steve returned to the parking lot, he found that Mable was still trying to get into her car. Two young adult males were hassling her by lightly slapping at the keys as she attempted to put them in the lock of her car. They kept calling her "Mama" and asking her to give them money. It appeared that they weren't intending to actually steal her purse but rather hoped to intimidate her into a "donation."

Since there was a security guard in the store, Steve went inside and asked him for help. He responded by saying, "Oh, some of those young kids have a knife or a gun. It isn't safe to get involved. I'll give the police a call." Steve was perplexed, thinking that the security guard had a gun and was presumably there to keep customers safe.

Knowing that Mable had high blood pressure and had to be under horrible stress, Steve said a quick prayer and headed back to the parking lot. He approached Mable and the two young adults, saying to them, "Hey, come on, knock it off." They stepped away from Mable and gave their attention to Steve, who was counting on the fact that most bullies lose their bluster quickly when confronted. They exchanged a few more words, some of which are X-rated, and then the young adults took off when Steve reminded them that the police had been called.

Fifteen minutes later, the police still had not arrived. Steve and Mable were sitting in her car talking. She finally said, "Well, I think I feel calm enough to drive now. This is the first time in my life I've truly felt in danger. My friends keep telling me that things are different and that it isn't safe to be out after dark, but I don't want to live my life governed by fear. That's just no way to live."

Governed by Fear?

Millions of people in North America join Mable in wanting to lead lives that aren't governed by fear. The reality, however, is that fear plays a major part in the way that we live. Many of us don't feel safe in parking lots at night, in hotel rooms, or even in our homes. The presence of a security guard or a police officer helps some of us feel safe, but there are persons of non-white ethnic background who do not find the presence of a police officer particularly reassuring. Also there are not enough police officers to enable us to feel safe all the time. The police who seemed slow to respond to the call from the security guard were in fact responding to another crisis in a different neighborhood at the time.

While we are intrigued by experiences like the one of Steve and Mable, such events are in fact not as common place as the media and politicians would have us believe. Fears about crime and safety make good news stories and provide wonderful forums for platitudes and promises from politicians. That doesn't mean that some of the dangers aren't real, but we need to recognize the reality that powerful interests are served by causing us not to feel safe. Steve began a workshop on hospitality prior to the September 11, 2001 attacks by reading these headlines from a newspaper:

LOCAL MAN KILLS THREE

14 TREATED FOR FIREWORKS INJURIES
GERMAN NAZI REPARATIONS COME TOO LATE

SENATOR FEARS HISTORY IMPEDES PEACE

STARR SPOKESMAN TO STAND TRIAL

PENTAGON PREPARES FOR MISSILE TRIAL

27 KILLED IN SPAIN COLLISION

HIJACKER HID GRENADE IN KIDS' BAGS

BELFAST TENSION HIGH AS MARCH PLANNED

There was also plenty of good news to report, but the most prominent headlines were ones reminding us how dangerous a place the world can be. Some local news shows have started segments with titles like "Focus on the Positive" and "Good News Spotlight." The very presence of these relatively short segments is a statement about the tone of the rest of the newscasts. Many of us lead more frightened lives than we realize.

While conducting a workshop on hospitality, Fred spent a delightful weekend as the guest of a couple who had a home on the side of a mountain. These were people of very high church involvement. Both of them have been volunteers in church sponsored disaster relief work and have traveled considerable distances to help people who are victims of floods, hurricanes, tornadoes, earthquakes, and fires.

They frequently open their home to guests who are present for church business in the area, and they are well known for their hospitality. Yet they have double-locked doors at both entrances to their house, and it takes two keys to get inside. Rather than a traditional screen door, they have a wrought iron door and then the main door. They keep their home locked all the time, even when they are there during daylight hours.

During the workshop, Fred talked about the role that fear plays in our lives. One of his hosts attended the workshop, and he and Fred shared in some interesting dialogue as a result. There are not many break-ins or crimes in the area in which this couple lives; but like large numbers of people in contemporary

North America, security has become a major issue to them. They live in fear of someone invading their space.

During the same workshop, Fred asked the guests how safe they feel and what is happening in terms of crime where they live. People have the perception that there is a high danger of their cars, homes, and businesses being robbed; and they are very concerned about the possibility of being assaulted.

That geographical area, however, has a very low crime rate. People in the workshop had very little personal experience of any kind of crime. One person had seen a person siphoning gas off a van in an office parking lot, but that was the only specific, recent instance of criminal activity that any of the ninety workshop participants could identify.

Fred has asked people about how safe they feel, how often they lock their doors, and how high the crime rate really is in workshops all around North America. Of course one expects people in major urban areas such as Chicago, Los Angeles, or Toronto to be concerned about crime and to keep their doors locked all the time. Fred has been surprised, however, to discover that the habits of people are little different even in relatively small towns with very high church-going populations. Many people in Harrisonburg, Virginia, Orrville, Ohio, and Goshen, Indiana, are just as obsessed with keeping doors locked as people in far more urban areas. As these words are being proofed the day before the manuscript goes to the printer, we have received word that a mentally ill factory worker in Goshen, Indiana, has wounded at least six people, killed one person, and then killed himself. People in Goshen have less to fear from crime than those in Los Angeles, but no place is completely safe.

Fear of crime is not the same as the fear created by the September 11, 2001 attacks. Here are some newspaper headlines from around North America on the day these words are being written:

U.S. TROOPS LEAD BID TO HALT TALIBAN PRISON UPRISING

BUSH WARNS IRAQ TO LET WEAPONS INSPECTORS BACK

PANEL SAYS U.S. ECONOMY ENTERED RECESSION IN MARCH

LAWYER TAPPED TO DIRECT VICTIM FUND

BUSH WANTS HUMAN CLONING BAN

LEAHY ANTHRAX LETTER REMAINS UNOPENED

We can lock our car doors, install home security systems, and form neighborhood watch groups to deter theft, vandalism, and bodily harm; but it's very difficult even to know what to do in order to protect ourselves against terrorism.

- Do we stop flying?

- Do we stop going to public places?

- Do we stop opening our mail?

- Do we purchase some kind of advanced filtration system for our household water?

- Do we purchase gas masks?

We've already suggested in the last chapter that it's important not to overreact–not to let ourselves become convinced we are in greater danger than we are. But those words are more easily written and spoken than converted to emotional reality. We cannot anticipate every possible manner in which terrorists could strike. We do not want to be held emotionally hostage. We also do not want to waste time and money on precautions that may make very little difference. At the time of this writing, the gas masks which are available only work effectively if custom-fitted to one's face and against particular kinds of inhaled substances. Most masks only work for thirty minutes. The movie star who bought gas masks for her five dogs is not protecting them as well as she hoped!

What Do We Fear?

The purpose of this book isn't to persuade you to abandon caution, to frequent parking lots late at night, or to leave your car and home unlocked. What we want to do is explore with you some of the ways in which fear and loneliness impact our lives and to consider the spiritual basis for a different view of other people and of the world. Take just a few moments to go through the list which follows and to rate your concern about each item from one to five. Let one represent "I have almost no fear of this" and five represent "I have a very high level of fear of this."

___ 1. Being on an airplane which is hijacked.

___ 2. Receiving anthrax or another disease through the mail system.

___ 3. Being in a public place (movie theater, shopping mall, athletic stadium) which is attacked in some way by terrorists.

___ 4. Having our water supply contaminated by terrorists.

___ 5. Being a victim of a bomb planted by terrorists.

___ 6. Having a disease like anthrax spread broadly by a crop dusting plane.

___ 7. Having a loved one become a victim of terrorism.

___ 8. Having a child who becomes almost immobilized over the threat of terrorism.

___ 9. Becoming almost immobilized myself over the threat of terrorism.

___10. Having a child grow up hating people of particular ethnic or national backgrounds because of terrorist reports.

___11. Finding that many people in our country have become intolerant of those of particular ethnic or national backgrounds because of fear of terrorism.

___11. Finding our nation involved in escalating war because of efforts to stop terrorism.

___12. Finding that our nation is guilty of violence toward people who are innocent in the process of trying to stop or prevent terrorism.

___13. Losing the lives of people I care about as they seek to protect others: fire fighters, police officers, and military personnel, for example.

___14. Having my identity stolen by someone who obtains my credit card number and social security number.

___15. Having my pocket picked or my purse snatched.

___16. Having my car stolen.

___17. Having my car broken into.

___18. Being a victim of an armed robbery.

___19. Having a burglary in my home while I'm gone.

___20. Having a burglary in my home while I'm there.

___21. Having my child or a child I know be kidnapped.

___22. Being assaulted by another person.

___23. Having someone I love be assaulted.

___24. Being sexually assaulted.

___25. Having someone I love be sexually assaulted.

___26. Being cheated or taken advantage of by a stranger.

___27. Being cheated or taken advantage of by someone I trust.

___28. Having a heart attack, cancer, or another life-threatening illness.

___29. Having someone I love have a heart attack, cancer, or another life-threatening illness.

___30. Being injured by a drunken driver.

___31. Having someone I love be injured by a drunken driver.

___32. Having drinking water made unsafe by pollution.

___33. Having the air made unsafe by pollution.

___34. Having my descendants inherit a world without safe water and air.

___35. Ending up without enough money to take care of myself in later years.

___36. Not having enough money to take care of those I love.

___37. Being in the midst of a tornado.

___38. Being in the midst of a hurricane.

___39. Being in the midst of an earthquake.

___40. Losing my home to a fire.

___41. Hurting someone by being careless in driving.

___42. Making bad financial decisions which cause serious problems for my family.

___43. Failing to respond to the needs of others as God would have me respond.

___44. Failing to do what God wants me to with my life.

___45. Dying and finding that I have disappointed God.

___46. Losing loved ones to death and still having years to go by myself.

___47. Doing something that diminishes the confidence my friends and family have in me.

___48. Finding I have been betrayed by a loved one.

___49. Becoming permanently disabled.

___50. Having a loved one become permanently disabled.

___51. Disappointing my employer or employees.

___52. Getting in trouble with the Internal Revenue Service.

___53. Being accused of a crime of which I'm not guilty.

___54. Having violence at a school in my community.

___55. Having a child of mine be harmed by drugs or alcohol.

___56. Looking foolish to other people.

___57. Appearing pathetic or lonely to other people.

___58. Looking like I can't control my emotions.

___59. Losing my marriage or a significant relationship.

___60. Losing my employment.

Obviously the list could be significantly expanded. Your greatest fears may or may not be represented in those sixty items. Try going through the list again and rating each item in terms of how likely you think it is to actually happen. There may well be some items on the list that have already happened to you and which have had significant impact on your life.

Bad things do happen to us. The world is not always a safe place, and no book or politician is going to make it safe. But how fearfully do we really want to live?

Fear and Loneliness

We have all experienced rejection because we were strangers to others. We know what it feels like to be ordered to present a driver's license and a credit card to get a check accepted at a store. We know the fear of having car trouble on the highway and not having anyone stop. We know the anxiety of trying to find our way around an unfamiliar neighborhood or city. In all these situations, we feel a fundamental loneliness.

In many respects, fear and distrust seem to have spread like a cancer in our land. Symbols of openness are disappearing from the North American scene as we barricade ourselves from strangers in an effort to protect ourselves and our possessions.

Electronic door locks on cars, double locks on house doors, security alarms, guard dogs, lobby guards, security officers, increased numbers of police, and the military are just a few signs of our deeply held fear of the stranger. We hide our money, lock our doors, chain our bikes, and look over our shoulders.

News reports of break-ins, break-outs, and blackouts feed our fears. We have come to view strangers more as potential enemies than as potential friends. We keep our eyes on our luggage and pocketbooks as we travel. We may feel sympathy for the hitchhiker or the stranded motorist, but most of the time we keep driving. When we park at a shopping mall, we lock our valuables in the trunk, away from the eyes of strangers. We are often victimized by our fears, instinctively avoiding persons who look or speak differently than we do.

All our social institutions have been affected by the growth of fear in our society. Churches, once known as havens of refuge and houses of prayer, now lock their doors to the very persons to whom they claim to minister. Our schools now post guards to protect students from students and teachers from students. Drug-sniffing dogs and metal detectors have become standard operating procedure in many schools. Many office buildings and large companies have significantly increased security, with some requiring registration of everyone who enters.

Certainly the statistics on violent crime over the past two decades justify a somewhat cautious approach to certain situations. The terrorist attacks remind us of our vulnerability. Yet it is one thing to live with a reasonable sense of caution and another entirely to have most of one's existence determined by fear. Instead of risking new possibilities for ourselves and the stranger, too many of us continue hiding behind our walls, lamenting the world's condition. By failing to come to know the stranger, we too often make that person an enemy rather than a friend.

That tendency has fed our loneliness. Large numbers of people feel shut off from others. People are cautious in new relationships, wanting to feel safe before revealing much of themselves or trusting too much in the other person. The events of September 11, 2001 have in some ways reinforced our fundamental bonds with one another, but they have also caused us to look at strangers with even greater suspicion.

Our loneliness is also fed by the technology of our time. E-mail has rapidly become one of the most frequently used means of communication, and in many respects it is a tremendous blessing. E-mail, however, is a significantly less personal means of communication than a phone call or a face-to-face conversation.

Increasing numbers of people find that they can comfortably work out of their homes. Steve does most of his work at a desk in the study of his home. E-mail, the fax machine, Federal Express, and the telephone enable him to stay strongly connected to those with whom he works. He and his colleagues in Christian Community and LifeQuest often exchange manuscript files and research data files by attachments to e-mail. It's a very effective means of sharing information, and it makes it possible to work easily with people hundreds or even thousands of miles away.

Steve's work also involves considerable travel and face-to-face interactions with his coworkers and others, so he continually feels strongly connected with people. It's easy to see, however, how the same style of work at home, for a person who did not travel much, could lead to a sense of isolation. The technology, on the whole, is a great blessing, but we need to be aware of the ways in which it can also feed loneliness.

A young adult who recently moved five hundred miles away from his home to accept a new job shared this perspective: "I'm surrounded by people, but I've never felt so lonely. There are two hundred people in the office where I work, and I know at least thirty of them by name already. But I don't do anything with them outside of work. I'm the new one in the department, and the others already have friends and a social life. People are nice to me, but I feel on the outside looking in.

"There are some people in the company that I only know through e-mail exchange and an occasional phone conversation. They work in other parts of the building or in another branch of the company, and there just isn't any occasion for us to get together. Sometimes I think about suggesting a face-to-face meeting with people in the same building, but then I think that would sound pretty needy.

"I live in a good-sized apartment complex, maybe eighty apartments and a couple of hundred people. My neighbors don't talk to each other. There are a few who make eye contact and smile, but they feel like the exception. I never thought of myself as introverted, but I don't know how to start getting to know people.

"I visited a couple of churches. I was the only young adult at both of them. I didn't especially mind that. People were friendly on the surface. The greeters and ushers shook hands with me, and visitors were introduced in the worship service at one of the churches. But people didn't remember who I was when I returned the next week.

"I know it will come in time, but right now I'm sorry that I moved here. I thought that I needed a new beginning away from my family and my college friends, but I'm not so sure now."

Then consider these comments from a woman who is eighty-two years old and has lived in the same neighborhood for the last forty-five years: "Everything in my life has changed in the last two decades. My husband has been dead for eight years now, but I'm still not adjusted to living alone. Every squeak in the house bothers me. My cat should be named Big Foot because he can sound just like a person coming up the stairs in the middle of the night.

"The whole neighborhood has changed. I know the names of the people on either side of me, and they seem nice enough. The young couple on one side of me makes a point every so often of saying, 'Now, you just call us if you need something.' I think they're sincere, and they'd help me get to the hospital in the middle of the night. But I can't call them just to say that I'm lonely. That would make me feel so foolish.

"It seems like my friends in the community and in the organizations I belong to keep moving into retirement homes or dying. I've been to four funerals this year. Each one makes me wonder how much longer I'll live, but I seem to keep going. My diabetes is under control, and my arthritis doesn't bother me too much. But I'm in danger of outliving everyone who is important to me. And it's just not easy to make new friends, especially at my age."

Then consider the perspective of a twenty-eight-year-old Muslim woman living in Chicago: "In some ways, I feel like I don't belong anywhere. Like some others my age in this country, I've chosen to reject the traditional dress of a Muslim woman. As I read the Quran, I just don't see that being an absolute obligation. Both men and women are urged to be modest, but the requirement in our time is mainly enforced on women. I wear the *hijab* [head covering] when I attend Islamic functions, but the rest of the time I dress as any other young American woman.

"My parents came here from Pakistan. They love this country and the freedom, but they are uncomfortable with my rejection of traditional Muslim expectations. They are somewhat bothered because I don't wear *hijab* and absolutely appalled that some of my skirts are so short. They don't approve of the whole concept of dating, and they are hurt that I don't want them to play a role in selecting a husband for me.

"But I'm not comfortable with everything about American society. I can't believe that a man who doesn't even know you will just come up to you and ask you out for a drink. If that person has never met you, then all he is going on is your physical appearance. He doesn't know you at all. And if you have a drink with him, then it won't be long before he starts suggesting that you sleep with him. No wonder so many people in this country are in bad relationships. I tell a man who approaches me like that to spend a year in an Islamic group I belong to, get to know me in that context, and then *maybe* I'll consider lunch with him.

"In my opinion, people in the United States and Canada have connected Muslims with terrorism for a long time. When the building blew up in Oklahoma City, the news media and the law enforcement people were immediately suspicious that a Muslim group was responsible. Then it turned out to be people who were native to this country. That was prejudice.

"Now that Osama bin Laden and his sick crew have done such horrible things, the rest of us who are Muslim suffer as well. I sometimes find myself not wanting to tell new people I meet that I am Muslim. They either look at me like I'm somehow responsible for what happened in New York and Washington, or they make these really patronizing comments about how open they are to people of other religions. What I would like is for them to be genuinely open rather than talk about being open.

"I know a great deal about the Christian faith; and like most Muslim people, I have tremendous respect for Jesus even though I don't view him in the same way as Christians do. But very few Christians know anything about the Islamic faith, and they don't seem to have any desire to learn more.

"So I don't feel all that well understood by my parents and older Muslim people, and I also don't feel like I fit in with the Christian and Jewish people who are the main ones with whom I interact on a daily basis. It wasn't easy before, and now Osama bin Laden has made it almost impossible."

Not all the fears that feed loneliness arc of terrorism, crime, or being taken advantage of by others. Some of the fears that affect us are more difficult to identify and sometimes awkward to acknowledge:

- The fear of appearing needy to others.

- The fear of others knowing how lonely we feel.

- The fear that others will not like us because of our age, appearance, economic status, race, or lifestyle.

- The fear of appearing foolish to others.

- The fear of acknowledging our own need for others.

Hospitality

The word hospitality is not new. We practice it in various ways as part of everyday life. At times, especially with those we already know and trust or know through others, we model it almost perfectly. We speak of Southern hospitality and understand the meaning of a "Hospitality Inn" sign. We use the word to describe persons who exhibit extraordinary graciousness. Being hospitable is for some the opposite of being rude. The word also evokes images of tea parties, pleasant conversations, and an aura of coziness.

The meaning of hospitality, however, goes deeper than those images. The experience and practice of hospitality lies at the very core of what it means to be a person of faith in the Christian or Jewish tradition. An old Hebrew proverb notes that "hospitality to strangers is greater than reverence for the name of God" [Robert E. Meagher in "Stranger at the Gate" in *Parabola 2*].

In the New Testament, the Letter to the Hebrews emphasizes the importance of hospitality: "Do not neglect to show hospitality to strangers, for by doing that some have entertained angels without knowing it" [13:2].

In our book *Widening the Welcome of the Church*, we defined hospitality and the stranger in this way:

> **Hospitality** is the attitude and practice of providing the atmosphere and opportunities, however risky, in which strangers are free to become friends, thereby feeling accepted, included, and loved. The relationship thus opens up the possibility for eventual communion among the host, the stranger, and God.
>
> The **stranger** is any person or group not known to the host. The host perceives that this unknown person or group has the potential for relationship as an enemy or as a friend.

Those definitions focused especially on the life of the church as the body of Christ and on the way in which hospitality should be practiced within congregational life. In this book, we want to move the discussion of hospitality out of the context of the congregation and into the very heart of the spiritual life for each of us. Consider this definition, as shared in the introduction:

Hospitality involves recognizing the presence of Christ in family, friends, coworkers, neighbors, and complete strangers. It means responding to others as we would respond to the presence of Christ in our midst.

The answer to fear is not to be found in the locks on our doors, in the promises of politicians, in increased police forces or prison populations, or in changed reporting by the news media. The answer to loneliness is not to be found in personal ads, in singles bars, in retirement communities, or in assertiveness training.

The answer to the fear and loneliness of our time comes in the development of the spiritual life and in a new way of seeing the people with whom we share our existence. Hospitality, fundamentally, is not a program for the church or even for self-improvement. It is a different way of living that sets us free to love and to be loved.

Those of us who live in the United States and Canada are well aware that our nations have become increasingly diverse. Depending on whose estimates you accept, there are between six and ten million Muslim people living in North America. Almost none of them are terrorists. Some, like the young woman quoted in the last section, have roots in countries like Pakistan; some are African-American; and most are persons of deep religious faith. Our hospitality needs to extend not only to persons who appear to be like us but also to those who are different.

Following the September 11, 2001 attacks, many Christian and Jewish people did reach out to those of the Muslim faith. President Bush took the initiative in urging people not to react negatively to their Islamic neighbors. Some churches invited Muslim leaders to speak, and some Christians stood guard at mosques to be sure no acts of violence were done. While a minority of United States citizens reacted negatively toward anyone of Muslim background, most recognized that Osama bin Laden was not representative of the Islamic faith or of the Muslim people.

Building a just and pleasant society, however, means more than the occasional guest speaker or isolated act of concern. Our hospitality needs to be sufficiently broad to embrace people of all backgrounds. Hospitality for Christian people is not simply a tool for evangelism–it is a way of life. It needs to be practiced with respect for persons of other faiths. The core changes needed in our society remain at the spiritual level.

Do not neglect to show hospitality to strangers, for by doing that some have entertained angels without knowing it.

Hebrews 13:2

Some Facts about Guns

- Every two hours in the United States, someone's child is killed with a loaded gun.

- If there is a gun in the home, the risk of suicide is five times greater.

- If there is a gun in the home, the risk of domestic homicide is three times greater.

- Over 50% of handgun owners keep their guns loaded, and over 50% do not keep their guns locked up.

- Firearms are often kept at home for protection, but they are seldom used for that purpose. Only 1.5% of those persons who were victims of home invasion crimes used a gun for self-defense.

- In 1998, of the 61 police officers who were murdered in the line of duty, 58 were killed with firearms. Six police officers were murdered with their own service weapons.

- There are over 200 million firearms in North America.

- A safety on a gun is a mechanical device–it can fail. Long guns are not "drop safe" even if they have safeties. The safety of a long gun normally blocks only the trigger but not the firing pin or the hammer.

Based on 1999 and 2000 information from the National Rifle Association and from United States Uniform Crime Reporting statistics.

Chapter Three:
The Spiritual Life and Hospitality

> **Concept:** Hospitality is not another self-improvement program. True hospitality is rooted in the spiritual life and transforms the way we view ourselves, other people, and God.

Melanie is a twenty-nine-year-old editor who loves mountain climbing. She grew up in Phoenix, Arizona, and learned from her father and her friends how to climb while a teenager. Now that she lives in New York City, mountains are not as easy to find; but she plans her vacations and an occasional long weekend to get as much climbing opportunity as possible. She has a special savings account to finance a trip to Mount Everest in three years.

She says that she would actually try scaling a couple of the skyscrapers in New York City, but local laws are designed to discourage such activities. She could climb a skyscraper and end up with a stiff fine and some bad publicity for her employer, both of which seem like too high a price for her.

"I don't actually think of it as dangerous," she says in describing her passion. "I've been climbing for so many years that I know my limitations, and I know the importance of doing it with people I trust. My boyfriend, who would like to be my fiancé, does feel that it's dangerous, though he's taken it up partly because it's so important to me and partly because he likes risk.

"It is more dangerous for him, because he's not as skilled as I am and doesn't always know his limitations. For him a lot of it is because he wants to share the experience with me, but it's also his own desire to overcome his fear. He was almost scared to death the first few times we simply scaled a wall at a sporting goods store. But overcoming fear is important to him.

"He'd been bungee jumping and sky diving before we met. Now those, to me, really sound dangerous. You're like totally dependent on your equipment. One mistake–you're a mashed potato. The equipment is important in mountain climbing; but I think you have a lot more control over what happens to you than in some other extreme sports. So I'm not scared of climbing, but there is no way you would get me to jump out of an airplane."

When asked why she does it, Melanie responded: "It's become part of me, part of my identity. I love the experience, the adrenalin rush, the beauty of being that high. I also like doing it with other people, the kind of bond you develop with others as you climb together. That's something I don't think you get from bungee jumping or sky diving, not in the same kind of way. And there's a spiritual dimension for me–there's a sense in which climbing makes me feel connected with the natural world and with God. My uncle is a Presbyterian minister, and he and I have talked about some of the ways being connected with nature, with the earth, brings us closer to God. I don't say that to most people, but that's part of what I feel."

We seek experiences that transcend our everyday lives in a multitude of ways. Interest in what are sometimes called extreme sports has risen significantly over the last decade. Participation has increased in mountain climbing, bungee jumping, sky diving, downhill mountain biking, and boxing. Some adventurous people like BASE jumping which involves parachuting off fixed objects like radio towers and bridges. BASE stands for Buildings, Antennas, Spans, and Earth!

The Sporting Goods Manufacturers Association says that in 1996 and 1997, the fastest-growing sport among teens and children in North America was in-line skating, which often means zooming down steep hills at speeds of 30 to 40 miles an hour. While not quite in the same category, hockey has enjoyed a tremendous increase in participation with amateur leagues appearing in cities around North America.

Not everyone who climbs mountains would call the experience spiritual, but Melanie's response is also not an unusual one. Many people, working at jobs that involve primarily their minds, crave opportunities that challenge them physically and that involve them emotionally at a deeper level than everyday life. Melanie doesn't think of climbing as dangerous in the way that many people, including the authors of this book, would. She does acknowledge that a certain amount of fear is healthy. Fear can be what motivates you to be sure your equipment is in good condition, to be sure you are well informed about weather, and to be sure you climb with people who are trustworthy. Too much fear can immobilize us, but a reasonable amount for rational reasons can keep us safe.

A young adult in the Army loved sky diving, but he also maintained that he would quit when he was no longer scared. He had observed that people who lose their fear with repetition sometimes start to get careless. That's when accidents happen, and sky diving accidents are fatal. When he reached the point that he was no longer frightened by these experiences, he stopped.

Seeking Experience and Meaning

We seek experience and meaning in a multitude of ways. Sports, travel, sex, drugs, and friendship can all be means of transcending our normal existence. There is in fact a hunger within us which pulls us to experiences that involve our bodies and our emotions as well as our minds. Many of us, however, do not seek to develop the spiritual life with the same energy that we put into gaining an education, earning a living, participating in sports, or even keeping the house clean. Thus the spiritual life becomes one part of who we are, but not the center of our being.

Much of the reason we are so driven by fear in our culture, that we are so uneasy around strangers, is that the spiritual life is not the main factor determining how we view other people and the opportunities available to us. We keep the spiritual life on the sidelines, ready to come into play if we attend a worship service or have a major crisis in our lives, but we don't develop it in such a way that it shapes how we live on a daily basis.

The events of September 11, 2001 were an awakening for many of us, causing us to ask the basic questions:

- For what are we really living? Why are we here? Is life something more than our work and the things we buy?

- What happens after death? Does life really continue for all those who were killed on September 11? Does it continue for the people who die each day in less spectacular ways?

- Does God protect us? Some lost their lives on September 11, but many were spared. What about the people who die from hunger or firearm accidents or drunk driving? Does God protect some but not others? Are we ourselves responsible for much of the suffering in the world?

- How can we develop deeper spiritual lives, a closer relationship with God? How can we develop a closer relationship with other people?

We should hope that we don't stop asking those questions. The questions have the power to pull us into more meaningful lives, including closer relationships with God and with other people.

Some people have mistakenly blamed the Islamic faith for the actions of Osama bin Laden and other terrorists. Those who hijacked and crashed the planes did apparently feel that they were doing the will of God and would be rewarded in Paradise. Those beliefs are repugnant to most Muslims who have been taught by the Quran and by the traditions of their faith that violence against the innocent is never justified. Those of us in the Christian tradition need to remember that our faith has been twisted and perverted to justify the Crusades, the Holocaust, and slavery. In an article in *Sightings*, William Schweiker reminds us:

> *No matter what beliefs and doctrines are held, as actually lived out by human beings, every religion is profoundly ambiguous. The religions are forces of life, justice, creativity and spiritual empowerment. But they are also forces of death, tyranny, ignorance, and moral failure. We cannot and ought not deny or ignore this fact.*
> [From *Sightings*, an online publication of the Martin Marty Center at the University of Chicago Divinity School, October 22, 2001]

The questions raised by the September 11 events should pull us closer to God and should also motivate us to think critically about what we believe and what we are taught concerning the faith. We have moved to dangerous ground when we use the

Christian faith to justify violence toward others or contempt for other religious traditions.

The authors are not intending to say that fear has no place in one's life. The concepts presented in this book are designed to liberate you from *unhealthy* fear. We all need to be free of the fear that blocks and distorts the quality of our relationships with others and that makes us view the world around us with excessive suspicion and lack of trust. That fear damages relationships and keeps us from viewing the world as God views it. There is another kind of fear that can be healthy, and that is the fear of God. Consider these verses of Scripture:

> *The fear of the LORD is the beginning of wisdom;*
> *all those who practice it have a good understanding.*
> Psalm 111:10

> *The fear of the LORD is the beginning of wisdom,*
> *and the knowledge of the Holy One is insight.*
> Proverbs 9:10

> *Commit your work to the LORD, and your plans*
> *will be established. . . . By loyalty and faithfulness*
> *iniquity is atoned for, and by the fear of the LORD*
> *one avoids evil."*
> Proverbs 16:3, 6

> *The spirit of the LORD shall rest on him, the spirit*
> *of wisdom and understanding, the spirit of counsel*
> *and might, the spirit of knowledge and the fear of the*
> *LORD. His delight shall be in the fear of the LORD.*
> Isaiah 11:2, 3a

> Jehoshaphat gave this warning to judges: *"Now, let*
> *the fear of the LORD be upon you; take care what you*
> *do, for there is no perversion of justice with the LORD*
> *our God, or partiality, or taking of bribes."*
> 2 Chronicles 19:7

> *Do not fear those who kill the body but cannot kill*
> *the soul; rather fear him who can destroy both soul*
> *and body in hell.*
> Matthew 10:28

> *His mercy is for those who fear him from generation to generation.*
>
> Luke 1:50

> *Meanwhile the church throughout Judea, Galilee, and Samaria had peace and was built up. Living in the fear of the Lord and in the comfort of the Holy Spirit, it increased in numbers.*
>
> Acts 9:31

Of course the word fear has a variety of meanings in those passages. We are not commanded to live in an immobilizing fear but rather to live out of a desire to know and to do God's will. The fear of God is closely linked to love of God and obedience to God.

As we discussed in the Introduction to this book, 1 John 4:17–20 promises that perfect love casts out fear; but perfect love is also directly related to how we view other people. Verse 20 reminds us that: "Those who say 'I love God,' and hate their brothers or sisters, are liars; for those who do not love a brother or sister whom they have seen, cannot love God whom they have not seen."

We are still striving for perfection in love, but most of us (at least in the experience of the authors) have not reached that goal. Thus a healthy fear of God, a genuine desire to know and do the will of God, should play a part in our spiritual lives. And that healthy fear of God, which motivates us to see the world differently, can transform our relationships with others. The search for meaning and experience is ultimately a search for God, who can be found on the mountaintops as Melanie does, but who can also be found within our hearts and around our lives each day of our existence. And the presence of God is continually coming to us in the strangers we encounter.

Lover of Strangers

The Greek word which is translated as hospitality, *philoxenos*, literally means "lover of strangers," which is similar to the Greek *philadelphia* or brotherly love. The concept of loving strangers is a foreign one to most of us. Far more of us have learned to be suspicious of strangers than to hold strangers in affection.

On a long airline flight, Fred met a delightful thirty-nine-year- old man who had grown up in the Jewish faith. Fred is normally the one to take the initiative in starting conversations with strangers, but this fellow traveler was the one to initiate their visit. He was fascinated to learn that Fred was a minister, and he shared with Fred that he had become a non-practicing Jew except for holy days. When Fred told him about the hospitality workshop that he was traveling to conduct, his new friend shared that his father had been the head usher in his childhood temple on Long Island. His father made sure visitors found a place to sit and people with whom to visit. His father would also see that these people received an invitation for a meal and a place to stay if needed.

Some of the spirit of that hospitality has obviously continued in this non-practicing Jew. He's on the board of a ski lodge, and he feels that he has a responsibility to help people feel at home at the lodge. He also practices hospitality in a less traditional, and some would even say unsafe, way: he travels a lot and always picks up hitch-hikers and helps them with food or money if needed.

Fred asked him why he picks up hitch-hikers, something that most people are frightened to do. He responded, "Because it's the decent, human thing to do." Fred suggested to him that his motivation may run deeper than he realizes: it may relate to his faith experiences early in life and to the example set by his father. Fred talked with him about hospitality from a biblical point of view and about Abraham as the patron saint of hospitality. Fred's new friend immediately identified with Abraham and remembered teachings from Hebrew School as he grew up.

When they arrived at their destination, the man accepted Fred's business card and said to him, "You are the first person in a long time I've been able to talk with about life issues–about what really matters. It seems like the conversations of my life are almost always just skimming along the surface."

Many of the conversations of life do skim along the surface, but Fred's Jewish friend is not alone in the desire to discover greater depth. Both he and Fred were blessed by their encounter on the plane. The Old Testament and the New Testament make it clear that strangers can be the source of great blessings.

Fred referred to Abraham as the patron saint of hospitality. Genesis 18:1-15 describes one of the most significant instances of Abraham's hospitality. Three strangers appear at the entrance of Abraham's tent, and he responds to them in a gracious manner. Biblical scholars (including Vawter, Von Rad, and Fretheim) agree that the three strangers are personages of Yahweh [God], though we are not clear in precisely what way. In *The New Interpreter's Bible*, Terence Fretheim offers this perspective: "From the narrator's point of view, Yahweh appears to Abraham at his home (v.1). From Abraham's point of view, however, three men stand near him (v.2). Yahweh has assumed human form appearing among the three men; the other two are angelic attendants" [Volume I, pp. 462-463].

Consider the text of Genesis 18:1-8:

> *The Lord appeared to Abraham by the oaks of Mamre, as he sat at the entrance of his tent in the heat of the day. He looked up and saw three men standing near him. When he saw them, he ran from the tent entrance to meet them, and bowed down to the ground. He said, "My lord, if I find favor with you, do not pass by your servant. Let a little water be brought, and wash your feet, and rest yourselves under the tree. Let me bring a little bread, that you may refresh yourselves, and after that you may pass on–since you have come to your servant."*
>
> *So they said, "Do as you have said." And Abraham hastened into the tent to Sarah, and said, "Make ready quickly three measures of choice flour, knead it, and make cakes." Abraham ran to the herd, and took a calf, tender and good, and gave it to the servant, who hastened to prepare it. Then he took curds and milk and the calf that he had prepared, and set it before them; and he stood by them under the tree while they ate.*

Abraham offers hospitality without being aware of the divine presence. That hospitality is consistent with the practice in the Ancient Near East and includes these elements:

- Abraham bows to them.

- Abraham offers them water, rest, and food–which they accept.

- The meal is prepared and includes a calf, which would have been reserved for a special occasion, and butter, which was greatly prized by the nomad.

- Abraham waits on them while they eat.

- The strangers did not reveal their identity nor did they offer any gift or payment prior to the meal.

In sharing the calf and the butter, Abraham and Sarah gave far more than custom required. They chose to treat the three men as honored guests, and they did so without expecting anything in return. As the story continues in verses 9-15, one of them tells Sarah that she will have a son. The fact that the gift of a child was promised can be seen as a response to their hospitality, but the promise of a son had already been made in the preceding chapter. The hospitality existed for its own sake, and Abraham has been lifted up as a model because of it. Had Abraham and Sarah refused hospitality to the strangers, they would have shut themselves off from the blessings God intended–not just the blessing of a son but also the blessing of God's presence.

The familiar New Testament words of Hebrews 13:2 are probably a reference to Abraham's experience: "Do not neglect to show hospitality to strangers, for by doing that some have entertained angels without knowing it." The New Testament provides us with a very strong example of hospitality in the parable of the Good Samaritan as recorded in Luke 10:29-37. The Samaritan did not evaluate the risk in responding to the person in need. The response was immediate, and it is a standard for our conduct–Jesus tells us to "Go and do likewise" [v. 37b].

The Presence of Christ

Matthew 25:31-46 presents an account very similar in some ways to that in Genesis 18. We are told to reach out to those who are hungry, naked, homeless, or imprisoned. When we show hospitality to such persons, it is as though the kindness is actually being shown to Christ:

> *"Lord, when was it that we saw you hungry or thirsty or a stranger or naked or sick or in prison, and did not take care of you?"*

> *Then he will answer them, "Truly I tell you, just as you did not do it to one of the least of these, you did not do it to me"* [25:45-46].

Fred likes to call Jesus the "Supreme Hospitalitor," for he laid down his life for others. The intention in Matthew 25 is to show the certainty of the end time and to answer the question of who will be judged as righteous. Persons who are hospitable to strangers are credited with those deeds as if the other person were Jesus Christ himself.

In this passage, Jesus makes it clear that we are not to reject the needy stranger; and Jesus shared that teaching knowing that he himself would be rejected and crucified. The stranger is to be welcomed, accepted, fed, and clothed. Welcoming the stranger opens the door to building relationships and developing deeper communion with one another and with God. Our relationships with others are transformed when we seriously consider the reality that we are encountering Christ in the other person. That should affect all of our relationships, every day of our lives.

The presence of Christ in others, of course, can be seen even more clearly in long term relationships; and we rightly cherish our parents, spouses, children, grandchildren, grandparents, and close friends. All of our closest friends, however, were once strangers to us. Recognizing Christ in others does not require a large set of shared experiences, though those experiences, clearly seen and understood, certainly deepen our bonds with others.

In *Reaching Out*, Henri Nouwen describes a visit from a person who had previously been a student in one of his courses. They sat on the ground together to talk, and then chose to sit in silence for a time. Nouwen felt a deep peace filling the space between them, and then his visitor said: "When I look at you it is as if I am in the presence of Christ."

Nouwen did not feel startled but simply replied: "It is the Christ in you, who recognizes the Christ in me."

"Yes," the visitor responded, "He indeed is in our midst." Then the visitor went on to speak words which Nouwen said were the most healing that had entered his soul in many years:

> *From now on, wherever you go, or wherever I go, all the ground between us will be holy ground* [p. 31].

The distance between ourselves and others begins to be transformed when we view it as holy ground, when we truly recognize the presence of Christ in all those with whom we share our days: family members, long-time friends, coworkers, neighbors, and strangers. The stranger in our lives today may be a long-time friend years later; or we may never again see the stranger, who nevertheless is a source of blessing to us.

Those on United Flight 93 on September 11 were strangers who acted together in order to protect other strangers. They had learned through cell phone conversations what had happened with the other hijacked planes. Some of them told those with whom they talked by phone that they were not going to let their flight become an instrument of destruction against others. We know from the flight recorder which was recovered that those passengers moved against the hijackers. The plane crashed into a field in western Pennsylvania rather than being used against another target. These strangers became bound to each other in a time of crisis, and they recognized their bond with the rest of humanity.

Those of the Quaker heritage sometimes speak of the divine spark in each person's breast. When we are open to the presence of that spark, it ignites and gains its own life. That spark is present even if we do not recognize it and even if we are afraid to name it as God within us. Others are more comfortable talking about the Holy Spirit as the divine presence within our hearts. Whatever name we place on the reality, that presence is in our hearts, in the hearts of those we have known for years, and in the hearts of those we may only interact with for seconds.

Some people who show hospitality are like Fred's traveling friend in not relating those acts of kindness to a spiritual motivation. The instruction of our childhood may affect our view of the world and our actions more deeply than we realize. At other times, the Christ within us, the Holy Spirit, the divine spark, may move us to great hospitality even though we fail to recognize the source of the desire to act in a loving way. The nonreligious can and do come to hospitality because of that unrecognized divine presence. It is possible to love one's neighbor without loving God, but God is nevertheless at the root of that love. If we crave a heightened spiritual life, then we need to open ourselves more fully to the presence of Christ within our lives. We then need to seek Christ's help in recognizing His presence in the lives of others, including the lives of strangers.

Guns to Ease Our Fears

But we are not accustomed to seeing Christ in the lives of strangers. Our fear of strangers and of crime continues to fuel a prosperous firearms industry. Most people who purchase guns for protection rather than for hunting would prefer not to be in a situation in which the gun had to be used, but the news media and other forces at work in our society have caused them to feel unsafe without a weapon. The information about guns, opposite the first page of this chapter, provides some reminders of the consequences of our placing reliance on firearms for protection.

We recognize that there will be many good people reading these words who take the faith seriously and who own handguns. Please consider the possibility that the weapon you have may end up used in a way you never intended. Firearms in fact are seldom used at home for protection, although many are purchased for that purpose. They are more likely to be used in three terrifying ways:

- As the cause of death for a child. Children do not
  understand firearms and are very curious about them.
  Television and motion pictures often depict violence
  in a way that is significantly different than real life. And
  children have an ability to find hidden firearms without
  parents realizing it until it's too late. Having a gun at the
  back of the top shelf of a closet isn't being safe enough.
  Even very young children find ways to climb. Having
  the weapon unloaded doesn't make it safe if there is
  any way a child can find ammunition, and 50% of hand-

gun owners keep their weapons loaded. Every two hours in the United States, a child is killed with a loaded gun.

- As the means of suicide. Statistical evidence continues to show that the risk of suicide is five times greater if there is a gun in the house. Obviously people take their own lives in a variety of ways besides firearms, but the ready availability and ease of use of a handgun increase the probability of someone taking that step.

- As the means of domestic homicide. Tragically, most people are in greater danger of violence from those they know and love than from strangers. The risk of domestic homicide is three times greater when there is a gun in the home. When feelings run strong and a gun is readily available, the temptation is more than some people can resist.

The statistics on guns we've shared at the start of this chapter and in this section come from 1999 and 2000 information from the National Rifle Association and from United States Uniform Crime Reporting data. The National Rifle Association argues persuasively that, if people are going to own guns, they need to be trained in how to safely store them and use them. The authors of this book have no argument with that and have respect for the educational work of the National Rifle Association.

But there is a more fundamental question which most of us need to ask: Do we need guns at all? If we are not hunters, why own a gun? Most of us do not have streets or neighborhoods that are so dangerous we need to be armed at all times. The presence of the gun is not very likely to protect us. The gun is far more likely to injure our children or grandchildren, to be the means by which a suicide is committed, or to be utilized in domestic violence.

Most police officers are considerably more knowledgeable and experienced in the use of firearms than the average gun owner. Yet in 1998, six of the 58 police officers in the United States who were killed by firearms were shot with their own service weapons. If police officers, who are highly trained and experienced, are that likely to be murdered by their own weapons, what does that say about the probability of the rest of us being harmed by our own guns?

One person who read this manuscript before publication made this observation: "This is a very strong argument against handguns, but what are the alternatives to help people feel safe if they do not have guns?" That is a fundamental question, and we cannot tell you that you will be safe from harm if you do not have a handgun. We do hope the information in this book will cause you to think carefully about the issues involved in owning a gun. Our argument against handguns for people other than law enforcement officers is based on three things:

1. The conviction that, for most of us, the dangers of owning a handgun are greater than any potential protection provided by the weapon.

2. The conviction that the world, while not entirely safe, is not as dangerous as news media, motion pictures, television programs, politicians, and others have caused us to feel. Reasonable precautions such as locks, alarm systems, and care in our routines can help protect us without bringing the danger of gun ownership.

3. The conviction that a deep spiritual life causes us to recognize the presence of Christ in others, including those we are tempted to fear. And a deeply held faith means that we ultimately depend upon God for our protection, knowing our Lord is with us no matter what we encounter.

Christ is in our spouses, parents, children, grandparents, and grandchildren. Christ is in our neighbors. Christ is even in the teenager who breaks into houses. How much danger are we willing to cause for others as the price for the security we feel from owning a handgun?

Help Me, Please

Hank, an exhausted executive, didn't leave his downtown office until 8:30 p.m. on a cold February evening. As he approached the almost deserted parking lot, Hank noticed a man getting out of an older car. The man and the car seemed to match each other, both clearly having had better days before the dings, scrapes, and rust of life left their marks.

As Hank headed for his own car, the man limped toward him. Hank hurried his pace, and the stranger hurried his, calling to Hank, "Could you help me, please?"

Hank thought it might be a person simply seeking a handout but was afraid the man might try to steal his billfold when he got close. Choosing to ignore him, Hank again increased his pace and tried to put confidence and determination into his walk. He used his remote control to unlock his car doors and turn on the lights, which immediately made him feel safer. He got into his car and locked the doors just before the stranger came even with him.

Looking up as the stranger tapped on his window, Hank reluctantly lowered it an inch to hear what the man said. "Could you help me, please?"

"I don't think so," Hank responded. "I don't have any money with me, so there's nothing I can do for you."

"I don't want money," the stranger responded and smiled. "My car won't start. I think all I need is a jump, and I have cables in my trunk. I've asked three people to help, and they've all refused. I called a wrecker service about coming to give me a jump, but they said it would be at least another hour. Is there any chance you could help me out?"

At close distance, the man looked like a mess; but he didn't look like a dangerous mess. The previous month, Hank's wife had been stranded in a supermarket parking lot with a similar problem without any help for two hours. Hank decided to take a chance.

The jump was all that the old car needed. As Hank started to leave, the stranger extended his hand and said, "I forgot to introduce myself. I'm Father Bill. I work at an inner city mission about eight blocks from here. Unfortunately, no one on staff there could leave to help me."

"You're a priest?!" Hank, also a Catholic, said in amazement. "Why didn't you say so? Why aren't you wearing a collar? I'd have helped you immediately if I'd known who you were. Your appearance frightened me."

"Well," Father Bill responded with another smile, "I am a priest, but a collar is a turn off to many of the people I'm trying to help. A lot of them have had bad experiences with the church. But wouldn't I have been just as deserving of help if I were the freeloader you first took me to be? Christ might be more fully present in a freeloader than in me."

"Which of these three, do you think, was a neighbor to the man who fell into the hands of the robbers?" He said, "The one who showed him mercy." Jesus said to him, "Go and do likewise."

Luke 10:36-37

Crime and Punishment

- If current incarceration rates in the United States remain unchanged, an estimated one out of every twenty people (5.1%) will serve time in a prison during his or her life.

- Based on current rates of incarceration, 28% of African-America males will enter a state or federal prison during their lifetime. The figure is 16% for Hispanic males and 4.4% for white males.

- Only 17% of federal inmates are in prison for a violent offense; 58% of them are imprisoned for a drug offense.

- 48% of jailed women reported having been physically or sexually abused prior to their incarceration.

- Over a third of all inmates report some kind of physical or mental disability.

- In 1997 and 1998, only a fourth of local jail inmates around North America were being held for a violent crime.

- 36% of convicted offenders were drinking alcohol at the time of the offense.

- Between 1980 and 1997, the population of California's state prisons increased by six times.

- It costs more to keep an inmate four years in a state or federal prison than to send the inmate to a private college.

1997, 1998, 1999, 2000 U.S. Department of Justice and State of California statistics.

Chapter Four:
Our Need for ~~Strangers~~ Guests

> **Concept:** Our tendency to spend time only with those we already know limits us and keeps us from receiving all the blessings God offers. We need to see the unknown person not as a stranger but as a guest sent from God to enrich our lives. Our outreach should extend to people of other ethnic backgrounds and religions.

Fred routinely makes new friends as he travels to conduct workshops and seminars. One of those new friends, Roberto, had lived for more than a year in an exclusive San Francisco suburb without knowing any of his neighbors by name. Roberto tried to strike up conversations with people, but he wasn't successful. It was a beautiful area in which to live, but people were cold toward one another.

Roberto wanted to live in a warmer, more friendly community, so he started looking for a complex that allowed pets. His theory was that people with pets would be more friendly and that there would be opportunities for conversation with people walking dogs. He was not disappointed with his new neighborhood! Pets constituted a safe topic for conversation, and the process of walking dogs provided many opportunities for interaction. People could sometimes move from the relatively safe topic of comparing pet experiences to talking about more personal things.

Animals, Nature, and People

Pets have a significant influence on many of our lives. Steve's Siamese cat, Tia, frequently sits on his desk, supervising his work. Often, a paw will gently touch his hand with the reminder that it's time to take a break from writing and share some affection with the supervisor.

When we encounter other people with pets, opportunities for conversation quickly open. We have an immediate point of connection; and at some level, many of us feel safer with people who have pets. It is as though the bond we form with pets and the gentleness required to make friends of them humanizes us in some important ways.

While pets can be quite demanding, sharing a home with a pet is less demanding than sharing a home with another person. Food, water, and affection are the main demands of a pet. Pets don't voice disagreements with us about religion, politics, motion pictures, or lifestyle issues. They don't chide us for overeating or undereating, and they never criticize us for failing to earn more money or for not attaining a higher status job. They don't aspire to a more upscale neighborhood, as they generally prefer to stay wherever we are right now. Most of them forgive us quickly when we treat them badly, and few of them harbor grudges. It's very difficult to maintain in any close human relationship the constancy of affection and devotion offered by a dog or a cat.

Our interest in animals extends beyond the domestic ones. Some of us feel more comfortable extending hospitality to animals than to people. We put out bird feeders and squirrel feeders, and we are delighted when we have a good response.

One can make a theological case for kindness to animals. Matthew Fox writes in *Confessions*:

> *Part of a Cosmic Christ theology is experiencing*
> *the Christ nature in all beings. I was gifted with*
> *such a friendship for seventeen years in the person*
> *of my dog, Tristan. . . . He was my spirit-guide*
> *for seventeen years, and after his death he has*
> *appeared in my dreams and those of others who*
> *knew him. I include him among a pantheon of spirits*
> *that have assisted me over the years* [pp. 155-56].

Some readers may find it difficult to accept Fox's identification of a dog as a spirit guide. Yet pets have a calming influence on us and often cause us to be kinder people. They slow us down when we are too busy, and their very presence can remind us of our priorities in life. Is it too great a stretch to think of them as guides sent from God to help us improve our lives?

But obviously there are dangers in carrying this too far. Fred has had a number of intriguing conversations with people living in the beautiful Pacific Northwest who talk about experiencing God so much in nature that they have no interest in the community of the church or any other religious organization. While one certainly can sense God's presence in animals and in other aspects of the natural world, we should not miss the way God is revealed in a community of faith.

A great many of us, at times, may prefer the presence of animals to the presence of humans, especially at the end of a long, busy day. That's not the same as a life in which pets have actually become more important than people and a substitute for developing new human relationships. It's also not the same as seeing God so much in the natural world that one is no longer able to see God as being at least as strongly present in the lives of other people.

We are all like Roberto in having a deep need for other people in our lives, even if we at times are reluctant to acknowledge that need. Those of us who have lived in the same neighborhood for decades and have many long established friendships may not feel the same need to meet new people as Roberto. That need is nevertheless present, even if we do not recognize it. While we gain rich rewards from long-established friendships, new relationships help us see life from different perspectives and offer us new insights. Christ may often seek to come to us and to enrich us through the introduction of new people into our lives.

The events of September 11 reminded many in the Christian faith of how little we know about those of the Islamic faith. One Muslim friend of Steve observed: "What most Christians know about Muslims comes from the newspapers or television when there are reports of some terrorist attack or of something controversial from the Nation of Islam." Try taking the quiz at the end of this chapter, and then read the commentary that accompanies the answers. If you would like an historic overview of the Islamic faith and a better understanding of why some Muslim people are hostile toward many European nations and the United States, read Karen Armstrong's excellent book *Islam* [Random House, New York, 2000]. For an interesting look at the Muslim faith and American culture from the perspective of a young Muslim woman, see Asma Gull Hasan's *American Muslims* [Continuum, New York, 2000].

The best way to truly understand the Islamic faith is to cultivate a friendship with a Muslim person. The United States and Canada do have some small communities with no Muslim residents, so building such a relationship is not an option for everyone reading this book. Many Christian people, however, go to school with, work with, or live near persons of Islamic faith. Many congregations have the possibility of seeking cross-cultural opportunities with Muslim organizations.

If we truly think about Christ being present in each person we encounter, then we realize that there is potential significance for every new relationship in our lives. The strangers we meet can be sources of great blessings and may one day be friends who are very important to us. God also brings other new people into our lives because there are blessings that we need to share with them.

Our tendency to spend time only with those we already know limits us and keeps us from receiving all the blessings God seeks to offer us. If we routinely avoid contact with strangers and try to minimize our interactions with people we do not know, we are in fact cutting ourselves off from meaningful experiences with the presence of Christ in those persons.

Bad Things Do Happen, But. . .

Bad things do happen. Crimes are committed every minute of every hour of every day. Natural disasters occur. And now we know that acts of terrorism can come without warning. As people of faith, however, we must continually strive not to let excessive fear rule our lives and separate us from others. Let's look at some of the ways we've been encouraged to be more fearful than is appropriate.

In his insightful book *The Culture of Fear*, Barry Glassner raises some fascinating questions:

> *Why, as crime rates plunged throughout the 1990s,*
> *did two-thirds of Americans believe they were soaring?*
> *How did it come about that by mid-decade 62 percent*
> *of us described ourselves as 'truly desperate' about*
> *crime—almost twice as many as in the late 1980s, when*
> *crime rates were higher?* [p. xi]

Politicians, the media, and others have created a culture of fear that affects all of us. In the United States, we pour a hundred billion dollars a year into criminal justice systems, primarily for police and prisons. Yet increases in persons imprisoned and in the size of police forces do not always correlate with reductions in crime.

Consider some of the statistics shared on the page opposite the beginning of this chapter. By the figures of the U.S. Department of Justice, if current incarceration rates continue, one out of every twenty people will serve prison time in his or her life. That's an incredible percentage. And the statistics show that black males and Hispanic males are more at risk than white males.

Many of those incarcerated are not there for violent crimes. In the federal prison system, only 17% are there for violent offenses. Only a fourth of local jail inmates are normally being held for a violent crime. One can logically ask why we are keeping in prison so many persons who do not pose any physical threat to society.

According to Barry Glassner, 75% of parents surveyed fear their children being kidnapped by a stranger. The truth, however, is that most missing children have been taken by a noncustodial parent or are fleeing abusive parents. There are claims of up to 800,000 missing children a year in the United States, but only 200 to 300 abductions are conducted by a nonfamily member and result in the child being missing for a long period of time or murdered [Glassner, p. 61]. Obviously 200 to 300 instances a year is excessive, but it doesn't justify the high sense of danger which most parents feel from strangers. The sad truth is that children are in the greatest danger from their own custodial and noncustodial parents–not from strangers. But the vast majority of parents are not abusive, and the vast majority of noncustodial parents would never take a child.

Racial fears also govern much of how we live and how we respond to strangers. In the United States, those racial fears are most strongly held by white people and are frequently directed at black people. Caryl Rivers, in *Slick Spins and Fractured Facts*, talks about the way media coverage of violent crimes emphasizes race. Through television news reporting, "night after night, black men rob, rape, loot, and pillage in the living room" [p. 161]. The same news coverage focuses far more on white victims than on black victims.

Media coverage of terrorist activities even before the destruction of the World Trade Center has often been quick to identify when Muslims were suspected of the violence. Perhaps it is "newsworthy" to identify the religious affiliation when that belief system contributes to the action taken. On the other hand, news reports do not consistently identify those suspected of attacks on abortion clinics as Christian, even though religious faith is generally a primary motivator of those actions. Far more crimes of all kinds are committed in North America by those of Christian faith than by those of Islamic faith.

Paranoia about homosexuality has also swept through North America. For many of the Christian faith, there are complicated biblical and theological questions concerning homosexuality. While many persons are convinced that the overall weight of Scripture does not condemn homosexuality, others point to a relatively small number of biblical passages and maintain that homosexual behavior is always sinful. There is room for persons of good conscience to disagree on this issue. Those theological questions, however, do not constitute a basis for fear of homosexual persons or an excuse for a lack of hospitality toward homosexuals.

There is no evidence that homosexual persons are greater threats to children than heterosexual persons. There is clear evidence that the disease AIDS affects both heterosexual and homosexual persons. Homosexual persons are in fact more likely to be the objects of hate crimes by homophobic people than to themselves be the cause of violence.

Many clergy, sadly, have fanned the flames of homophobia by continual harangues on this issue. They've caused some people to fear that the United States and Canada are in danger of being taken over by a homosexual agenda and that the church itself is in danger of being taken over by homosexuals. Some churches have felt it important to develop clear statements which exclude persons of homosexual behavior, and sometimes simply homosexual orientation, from membership and involvement. Yet the reality is that homosexual persons are no different than others in wanting acceptance and in not going places where they are not welcome. Any church which encourages contempt for homosexual persons need not be concerned that homosexuals will become members.

There is considerable evidence of homosexual persons wanting to have their rights protected by the laws of society. There is likewise evidence of them wanting to be accepted and affirmed by others, just as heterosexual people want to be. There is no evidence of a homosexual agenda which threatens the well-being of the dominant heterosexual society. Our fears too often overwhelm our logic and our decency.

Fear can have many consequences beyond our own uneasiness and damaged relationships. Our fear can cause hatred, and hatred can lead to evil. When we fear persons of another race or of another sexual orientation or of a different background, that fear can turn to hatred. The forces of evil are drawn to fear and prey on it. Matthew Fox shares this counsel in *Confessions:*

> *These evil forces prey on fear. How important!*
> *So much fear runs the world, that of fundamentalism*
> *for example. Only when fear lets the evil in does*
> *evil happen. Thus, the importance of spirituality–*
> *to build the strength, the big heart (courage)–*
> *based on faith, i.e., trust, which is the opposite*
> *of fear–that combats evil successfully* [p. 192].

The fundamentalism which Fox uses as an example can exist within all religious traditions including Christian, Jewish, and Islamic.

The words of Leonard Pitts Jr., in his September 29, 2001 column in *The Miami Herald,* remind us that fundamentalism played a role not only in the attacks of September 11 but also in the interpretation of them:

> *After all, the men who hijacked the planes thought they*
> *acted at the behest of Allah. And Jerry Falwell, a*
> *Christian minister, claims their attack represents God's*
> *verdict on the ACLU and other bogeymen of the right wing.*

It's important to note that Jerry Falwell did later retract and apologize for the strong statements that he made immediately after the terrorist attacks. The reality, however, is that fear of others and of challenges to a fundamentalist faith no doubt played a major role both in the terrorist attacks and in the reactions people like Falwell had to them.

In Ephesians, we are reminded of the reality of evil forces in the world. "For our struggle is not against enemies of blood and flesh, but against the rulers, against the authorities, against the cosmic powers of this present darkness, against the spiritual forces of evil in the heavenly places" [v.6:12]. Our fear strengthens those evil forces and closes us to the blessings God wishes to give us through other people.

The Feathered Guest

Birds frequent the Clapps' back yard because of a bird feeder, a bird bath, and a number of flowers and plants. On a summer evening, when Steve was in Ohio visiting with Fred, Steve's wife Sara discovered an unusual feathered visitor. The bird seemed to be hiding in the cage that supported a tomato plant. The creature was brightly colored and was larger than a parakeet but smaller that any parrot she had seen. Sara offered food and water which the bird accepted, though it drank very little.

The bird was still there when Steve came home around midnight. They both expected it to leave in the morning, but they were wrong. They offered more food, and it proved tame enough to jump onto Sara's back, a spot from which it was not inclined to move. They didn't have a cage at hand, or they might have captured it for its protection. Its wings had been clipped, however, so it did not appear likely it was going to go over the tall fence that surrounds their yard. Flying seemed difficult enough for it that Steve and Sara were a little surprised it had made it into their yard. Sara suggested that perhaps their St. Francis statue had drawn it.

It was a beautiful bird, but neither of them knew what kind. They called the zoo, which was not missing any birds. They called the animal control office, which didn't have any current reports of missing birds but did help them identify their guest: it was a cockatiel. They called people in the neighborhood, trying to find the bird's home. They called the newspaper and placed an advertisement searching for the owner.

They felt a little foolish calling the zoo and animal control without being able to identify the species of the bird, but people at both places were kind and helpful. *The Fort Wayne Journal Gazette* and *News Sentinel* placed the advertisement without charge, which is a standard policy of those papers for FOUND pets. Neighbors phoned other neighbors to seek the bird's owner. Two people who had lost cockatiels called, but this particular bird did not belong to either of them. The bird's owner was not found, causing one to wonder if the bird was simply set free, which is not a good plight for a bird so thoroughly domesticated.

The bird's situation elicited kindness not only from Steve and Sara but also from many others. Through the efforts to help the bird, Steve and Sara had a number of very interesting interactions with other people and learned some things about birds they would not have known otherwise. The bird which appeared in their yard as a stranger became a guest and a source of blessings. That's what happens with strangers of the human variety too.

Margaret and Frank never felt comfortable around homosexual persons and felt homosexual behavior was sinful. Bill, their only child, lived on the opposite side of the country and only came home twice a year: once at the time of his birthday and once for Christmas. Margaret was afraid of flying, so she and Frank never made the cross country trip to visit Bill at his home.

Then came the Christmas that Bill came home and shared two pieces of information which were hard for Margaret and Frank to accept. First, he told them that he was homosexual. Second, he told them that he had AIDS. His physical appearance told them that he probably did not have long to live.

Margaret and Frank loved Bill dearly, but they didn't know how to respond to this news. After Christmas, Bill returned to his own home across the country, with Frank and Margaret promising that they would come visit him and meet his partner. Bill had not brought his partner home for Christmas, fearing that it would be more than his parents could handle.

But Margaret and Frank never made the trip. Their son died two months after Christmas. Their son's partner, Evan, arranged to have the body shipped back and returned himself for the funeral, which Bill had wanted to be conducted by the minister of his parents' congregation. Evan arranged to stay in a motel, and Margaret and Frank were relieved. They felt slightly guilty for not inviting Evan into their home, but their feelings were too ambivalent to extend the hospitality.

They had polite words with Evan at the funeral home and after the funeral service. They made vague promises to "keep in touch," but all three of them knew they wouldn't be doing that.

The one consolation Margaret took was that she believed there was nothing else as awful as having a son die of AIDS that could ever happen to her. She was wrong. Only a few weeks later, her husband died in an automobile accident. Margaret was devastated. Within the space of only a few months, she had learned that her son was homosexual, had her son die, and then had her husband die.

Margaret's faith in God was deep, and that was what pulled her through the difficult days that followed. In talking with her minister, she confessed that she felt deep regret for not having visited with her son when he was so ill. She wished that she had understood more of what was happening in his life and why he was homosexual. She also wished she knew more about AIDS. But, she told her pastor, "There's nothing to be done now. I can't learn anything more about my son."

"Perhaps not," her pastor responded, "but you could learn more about someone else who is having a similar experience. There's a hospice program in town that needs volunteers to help people who are dying of AIDS and don't have family to help them."

"I could never do that," Margaret protested. "I would be far too uncomfortable. And those people wouldn't want help from someone like me."

"Those people, Margaret," her pastor counseled, "are not as different from you as you may think. Here's a phone number."

She put the phone number on the bulletin board beside her kitchen telephone. She thought about throwing it away several times over the next three weeks, but something kept stopping her.

Then she read a morning devotion with this line: "Risk stepping outside your comfort zone. God is waiting for you with great blessings just the other side of that zone." She dialed the number and attended an orientation for volunteers.

Margaret was assigned to Zack, a young man only a couple of years older than her son had been. Zack did not have long to live, but he did not want to be part of the residential hospice program. He wanted to stay in his own home. A nurse's aide helped him medically, but he needed someone to shop for groceries for him and to help with household tasks. Margaret was very uneasy about the arrangement, but Zack reminded her just enough of Bill that she kept going back to his apartment.

When she had begun to feel a little more confident around Zack and a little less afraid of visiting with him, she asked him why he wasn't receiving help from a partner or from his parents. She learned that his partner had already died of AIDS and that Zack had taken care of him. Zack cried as he told her that his parents simply could not accept his homosexuality and wanted nothing to do with him. Margaret left the apartment that day and collapsed in tears on the front seat of her car, filled with compassion for Zack and horribly afraid that Bill had felt similar rejection from herself and from Frank. She prayed to God for forgiveness for her difficulty in fully accepting her own son. As she prayed, she found her mind drawn again and again to these words: "But you can accept and love Zack."

And she did. She wanted to learn everything she could about Zack. He was open in talking to her, and she soon found herself pouring out her heart to him. She brought pictures of her husband and son. She told him about Bill's childhood, and Zack told her about his own. As they continued sharing over the next few weeks, she began to understand how much Zack had not wanted to be homosexual. To him, it did not appear a matter of choice; it was how he was programmed. Margaret had never been able to accept that view of homosexuality, not even in Bill, but she struggled to understand as Zack tearfully shared the inner battles he had experienced.

Zack died four months from the date of Margaret's first visit to his apartment, and he died holding Margaret's hand. He had no will or living trust, and he had no money left. His parents refused to have any part in the funeral, so Margaret planned it and paid for it.

The day after Zack's funeral, she made two phone calls. The first was to the hospice center to request another volunteer opportunity. The second was to Evan, to see if he would come spend Christmas in her home so they could talk together about Bill.

God is with us even in the midst of great tragedy. And strangers are often the means through which God brings healing and blessings to our lives.

Strangers and Blessings

"Do not neglect to show hospitality to strangers, for by doing that some have entertained angels without knowing it" [Hebrews 13:2]. The story of Margaret and Zack is powerful, but it is not unique. Lives are transformed on a continuing basis through interaction with strangers:

- Bob, a member of the Ku Klux Klan, experienced car trouble on a deserted stretch of highway late at night. He was at first terrified when a car with three black teenagers stopped by his. The three teens, however, were filled with goodwill and cheerfully repaired his car for him. Bob found himself genuinely enjoying the interaction with them and being impressed by their intelligence and warm sense of humor. They refused to accept money for their help, and the last words he heard were one of them saying, "Hey, God be with you, man." His life was changed.

- Betty was eighty years old and had never cared very much for young children. She had been an only child and had never married. She was more than a little dismayed when the house next to hers was purchased by a family with three young children. The second day after they moved into the house, her fears were confirmed when she saw two of the children walking through her flowers. She yelled at them, told them to never again come onto her property, and then phoned a fence company. The third day, the two children appeared at Betty's door with a plate of cookies, a bouquet of flowers, and profuse apologies for damaging her flowers. The fourth day, the children's mother came and invited Betty to join them for supper. The fifth day, Betty called the fence company and told them not to come.

- Harry was a widower and lived alone. He dearly loved his adult children, but they and their families lived hundreds of miles away. He woke up one morning feeling particularly lonely and discouraged. He started to take his heart medicine and then thought, "Why bother? What am I really living for?" He walked to the 7-11 store three blocks from his house to buy a newspaper and a cup of coffee. A new clerk, a Muslim woman, was working at the counter and cheerfully introduced herself to him. The store was not busy, and he found himself visiting with her for ten minutes. He told her about his children, and she said, "I'll bet they miss you as much as you miss them." Harry went back to his home and took his heart medicine.

- At the age of fourteen, Brian made his third appearance before the same judge. This time the judge ordered him to participate as a volunteer at a soup kitchen run by a Catholic parish. Brian discovered that the soup kitchen was supervised by Alice who was seventy-two years old and was not about to be intimidated by someone who was fourteen. At first he feared her. Then he hated her for making him do tasks over repeatedly until he did them right and for making him apologize when he was rude. But then he found his feelings for Alice beginning to change because, in spite of his difficult behavior, she really seemed to like him. Soon Brian realized that he looked forward to going to the soup kitchen, and he began to find himself talking with Alice about what was happening in his life.

- Mary Jo was eighty years old and suffered from both high blood pressure and diabetes. She moved to a new community to be close to her son, but that meant she had to get a new physician. She had been very fond of her former physician and had also felt comfortable with his understanding that she wanted no extraordinary measures taken to preserve her life. Her new physician was from the Middle East, and she liked him immediately. She continued to be concerned, however, about whether or not he would share and understand her views on life and death. She brought the subject up at a routine office visit and discovered that he was Muslim. He told her that he did not generally tell people about his religion because it made them feel uncomfortable. Then they talked about their views of life, death, and the life to come. Mary Jo found that they were kindred spirits, feeling almost exactly the same about the preciousness of life and the importance of recognizing that this life is not the end of existence. They became blessings to each other.

How might your life be transformed by interaction with people you do not yet know? What impact might you have on the life of someone else? Who are the angels you might be asked to entertain?

> *Try taking the Quiz on the Islamic Faith which appears on the next page and study the answers which follow. Remember, however, that a short description of the Christian or Jewish faith would involve considerable oversimplification. The same is true of the information shared here.*

A Quiz on the Islamic Faith

True or False? Answers are on pages 86 and 87.

___ 1. The Islamic faith began with the revelations of the Quran received by the Prophet Muhammad at Mecca.

___ 2. The Islamic faith teaches people to build a private fortune as a sign of God's blessing.

___ 3. The word *islam* means paradise, and a *muslim* is a person ready to claim it.

___ 4. The Quran denies women rights of inheritance.

___ 5. The Quran permits polygamy.

___ 6. Malcolm X founded the Nation of Islam.

___ 7. The European invasion of the Islamic culture and the modernization process have created many problems for Muslims.

___ 8. Worldwide there are about twenty million Muslims.

___ 9. Muslim people are expected to pray five times a day.

___10. *Hijab* is the head covering worn by many Muslim women.

___11. *Jihad* means a holy war for Allah.

___12. The Quran has a chapter devoted to Mary, the mother of Jesus.

___13. Many people in prison convert to the Islamic faith.

___ 14. Almost all Islamic people disagree strongly with the teachings and actions of people like Osama bin Laden.

Answers to the Quiz

1. True. Those revelations were received in Mecca in the year 610 during the feast of Ramadan. Muhammad did not see himself founding a new religion. The religions of his people prior to that time would be described by most as "pagan," but some people did believe in one god called al-Lah, which means "the God." Muhammad thought he was bringing this faith in one God to the Arab world, which had not had a prophet before.

2. False. Muhammad thought it was wrong to build a private fortune and ignore the needs of the poor. Islam has always emphasized creating a just society. Muhammad was distressed that his tribe had people making money at the expense of the poor. He would certainly not be pleased at the concentration of wealth in the hands of a few in Afghanistan with so many others living in poverty.

3. False. *Islam* means surrender, and a *muslim* is a person who has submitted his or her entire being to Allah including "his demand that human beings behave to one another with justice, equity, and compassion" [Karen Armstrong, *Islam*, p. 5].

4. False. The Quran (the sacred Scripture of Islam) gives women the right of inheritance and divorce. Muhammad was an advocate for the emancipation of women.

5. True. Many Muslim men were killed in wars, and life in the Arab world was difficult for women who were not married. Men were permitted to have up to four wives. Before judging this view as primitive, Christians and Jews would do well to remember the wives and concubines of Solomon.

6. False. It was founded by Wallace Fard, who taught that white people were evil. Although Malcolm X did bring considerable respect to the Nation of Islam, he became disillusioned with the organization. Malcolm X took his followers into Sunni Islam by founding the American Muslim Mission. This is a larger and more orthodox organization than the Nation of Islam but gains less media attention.

7. True. The Islamic culture found it difficult to deal with the rapid rate of change and technological advancement which

accompanied European culture. Many of the colonists had contempt for the Muslim people and felt themselves racially superior. Muslim society did not view modernization and the lack of respect for the poor as progress.

8. False. There are at least a billion Muslim people around the world. Six to ten million live in North America. Most Muslims belong to either the Sunni or the Shiite sects, with Sunni being the largest. Sunnis and Shias are in agreement on the major beliefs of Islam. They follow the teachings of Muhammad, believe in the Quran, and accept the "Five Pillars of Islam."

9. True. Praying five times a day is one of the Five Pillars. The other four are belief in the statement "There is no god but God, and Muhammad is his prophet"; giving alms to the poor; abstaining from food, drink, and sex between sunrise and sunset during the Islamic month of Ramadan; and making a pilgrimage to Mecca once in a lifetime if possible.

10. True. The Quran does not, however, have a clear require-ment that women wear a head covering. The Quran teaches modesty for both men and women. The covering of a woman's head has become a part of Muslim tradition, but many younger women in North America do not practice it.

11. False. The word *jihad* means struggle or effort. It especially refers to efforts to bring about positive change and repentance from evil for individuals and religious communities. It can describe a religious war, but that is not the primary meaning. *Jihad* has come for many Muslim people to mean a struggle against the influence of western culture.

12. True. The Quran describes the virgin birth of Jesus. Islam maintains that Muhammad was the last in a line of prophets including Adam, Abraham, Moses, and Jesus.

13. True. At one time, the Nation of Islam had tremendous growth through the conversion of African-Americans who were imprisoned. Today most of the 35,000 prison converts a year are to Sunni Islam rather than the Nation of Islam.

14. True. While many Islamic people are distressed by Western culture, Osama bin Laden's teachings and actions are considered evil.

Keeping Safe in Thunderstorms

- If you are outside and can hear thunder, then you are close enough to be struck by lightning. Find shelter.

- Do not take shelter in small sheds, under isolated trees, in convertibles, or near fences or poles. Seek a sturdy building.

- If you are in the woods, take shelter under the shorter trees.

- If you are outside and feel your hair stand on end or your skin tingle, squat low to the ground and place your hands on your knees with your head between them. You want to minimize contact with the ground and make yourself the smallest possible target.

- Get out of boats and avoid water.

- Avoid telephone lines and metal pipes, which can conduct electricity.

- Do not take a bath or shower.

- Turn off air conditioners. The power surge from lightning can overload the compressor.

- Unplug appliances not needed for weather information.

Based in part on information from the New York State Disaster Preparedness Commission.

Chapter Five:
Prayer and Hospitality

Concept: True hospitality is only possible when our lives are grounded in prayer and intimately connected with God. Prayer can transform the fundamental way in which we view the world around us.

What happened to the cockatiel who was introduced in the last chapter? Steve and Sara Clapp finally found a cage for the bird and continued their unsuccessful campaign to find its owner. Their feathered guest, however, had other plans.

The weather was good, and they left the caged cockatiel on a deck, thinking that it was pleasant for the bird to be in the sunlight. They also were afraid that, if they brought the cage into the house, their cats would terrorize the bird. The cage they used to house the cockatiel was one that had been used in house training their dog. The bars looked narrow enough to confine the cockatiel who initially made no serious effort to escape. The bird ate well and interacted pleasantly with Steve, Sara, and their curious dog.

But the cockatiel apparently decided he (or perhaps she) had experienced enough of their hospitality and managed to escape from the cage by some kind of unwitnessed maneuver. They searched the neighborhood and left out special cockatiel food for two days, hoping the bird would return. With crows and cats patrolling the neighborhood, they didn't feel the rather friendly bird was likely to survive a long time.

Thus Steve can't provide a happy ending to the story of the cockatiel. He simply does not know what happened to the bird. In wonderful hindsight, he wishes that he had brought the cage into his study and kept the cats shut out of the room. Steve and Sara had been unsuccessful in finding the bird's owner, but their inquiries had resulted in more than one offer of a good home for the bird. Sara thinks it may have been a mistake to cage the cockatiel while searching for its owner. The bird seemed to be enjoying their yard and interacted pleasantly with them. Perhaps the bird would have continued to stay in the yard until a home had been found if they had not put it in a cage.

While hospitality usually produces blessings, not every inter-action with strangers will have a happy ending. The cockatiel certainly was a blessing to Steve and Sara in various ways, and presumably the bird benefited from the food and attention it received. Steve and Sara cannot help wishing that there had been a different ending to the story.

Hillary and Brad reached out to a couple their age who moved into their neighborhood. As soon as the movers had finished unloading, Hillary took a plate of cookies to their new neighbors. Amy and Ted were delighted by her welcome, and the two couples began to develop a relationship. Both households had young children who became friends.

Amy and Ted started attending the same church as Hillary and Brad. While Hillary and Brad were aware that money seemed a little tighter for Amy and Ted than for themselves, that did not concern them; in fact, Hillary and Brad tried to find small ways that they could be of help, especially by sharing clothing their children were outgrowing.

Then they started noticing that Ted wasn't leaving for work as early in the morning as he had been, though he was gone much of the day. After a week of this new pattern, Amy confided to Hillary that Ted had been fired and was looking for a new job.

A week later, Ted approached Brad and asked for a small loan to help with groceries and their electrical bill. Amy, like Hillary, had only a part-time job because of the age of their children; and that pay didn't stretch very far. Brad was glad to help and also suggested that Ted seek an interview with Brad's employer. Over the course of the next month, Hillary and Brad loaned over a thousand dollars to Amy and Ted. When they felt that they couldn't advance more money, they referred Amy and Ted to the pastor of the church who helped them from the emergency fund the church maintained for such needs. Ted and Amy didn't have family to whom they could turn for help, and they were very grateful for what Hillary, Brad, and the church did for them.

Ted did get a job with Brad's company, largely through Brad's influence. With his first paycheck, Brad started repaying the money borrowed from Hillary and Brad and said that he wanted to repay the church as well, though the pastor had made it clear that no repayment was expected.

Six weeks later, Ted was fired. Brad learned from Ted's supervisor that Ted had lacked the flexibility needed and that, when pushed to change, he had shown a strong temper, something Hillary and Brad had never encountered. Hillary and Brad were determined to remain friends and had them over for dinner the weekend following Ted's termination.

Over the next three months, Ted gained and lost another job; and Ted and Amy's debt to Hillary and Brad increased by another thousand dollars. The pastor also advanced more money to them. Amy tearfully acknowledged to Hillary that Ted's temper was a problem from the beginning of their marriage. The first three years had been reasonably good ones, because Ted worked for a small business owned by his father. The father made allowances for his son's temper and once fired another employee who couldn't get along with Ted. Then Ted's parents were killed in an automobile accident, and Ted had not been able to keep the family business going.

Amy maintained that Ted had never been abusive to her or their children, and Hillary and Brad never saw a direct display of Ted's temper. The situation, nevertheless, felt increasingly awkward as Amy and Ted's financial situation deteriorated, and Holly and Brad felt unable to do anything further.

The problem was resolved when Ted got a job in another city. This time they moved themselves, using a rented truck. Brad, Hillary, and some others from their church helped in the move. Ted and Amy promised Hillary and Brad that they would stay in touch and would eventually repay the money they had borrowed.

They did repay about half the money, and Amy and Hillary communicated by e-mail for several weeks. Then Amy said in an e-mail that Ted had been fired again and that they weren't sure what they were going to do. The e-mails stopped coming, and there were no more payments on the money which was owed. Hillary and Brad tried to call, but the phone number was no longer in service. Then Hillary and Brad sent a letter, telling Amy and Ted to forget about the debt but to please keep in touch with them. The letter was returned by the postal system with "NO FORWARDING ADDRESS ON FILE" stamped on it.

Hillary and Brad showed genuine hospitality and compassion to Amy and Ted. Their congregation and pastor also showed compassion and a willingness to help. Hillary and Brad felt more let down by the failure of Amy and Ted to stay in contact than by the fact that the money did not get repaid. They were not sorry for what they had done to help these strangers who became friends.

Not Optional and Not Safe

In our book *Widening the Welcome of Your Church*, we titled the first chapter: "Hospitality: Not Optional and Not Safe." We feel that the Old and New Testaments make it clear that Christian people are to practice hospitality. It is not optional. When we fail to practice hospitality, we are closing our hearts to the blessings God wishes to share and to the presence of Christ in other people.

Perhaps the most significant New Testament admonition about hospitality comes in the parable of the Good Samaritan, which was told by Christ to answer the question "And who is my neighbor?" [Luke 10:29b]. The Samaritan "was moved with pity" [v.33] for the man who had been injured, helped him, and arranged for his continuing care by the innkeeper. Our obligations are not just to the people we already know.

But the practice of hospitality is not always safe. Someone we choose to befriend may turn out to be manipulative or dishonest. Some may be essentially honest but have such serious problems, like Ted and Amy, that our efforts do not have the result we want. We may occasionally extend hospitality toward those who will reject us. We may find that the practice of hospitality leads us into contact with persons we would otherwise have avoided.

Following the example of Christ has never been a guarantee of a problem-free existence. Reaching out, as Christ would have us do, does not free us from pain and suffering. We may see the pain and sorrow of the world more clearly than ever as we attempt to view others as Christ would. As we live in a time of greater fear, it is important for us to examine the attitudes with which we look at others.

A friend of Steve's who lives in New York City shared this perspective on the events of September 11, 2001: "Initially it was like the entire city was transformed. On September 11, ordinary people reached out to those they did not know with acts of heroism and compassion. There was an enormous outpouring of concern and donations. Under the threat of attack from the outside, we let our guard down and became less suspicious of one another. But old habits are not easily abandoned. As the days and weeks go by, I see people reverting to the guarded, avoid eye contact way of walking and conducting business that was taken for granted before that terrible day. We are still kinder to each other than we were before the attack, but we've lost ground."

Muslim people and those who even appear to be Middle Eastern are likely to think our society has become crueler rather than kinder. A young adult who has dark skin and a Middle Eastern sounding name has stopped traveling by airplane. He doesn't exactly blame the airline employees and the security personnel for viewing him with such suspicion, but the more thorough searches which he and his luggage routinely receive are extremely unpleasant. Like his grandparents and parents on both sides of the family, he was born in the United States. He and the rest of his family are Roman Catholic, not Muslim; and he has one uncle who is a priest. But he is judged by his appearance and his name not only by airport personnel but by many others. "An occasional apology and a smile would make the security process less dehumanizing," he reflected. "And I don't understand why other travelers cast suspicious looks my way. The airport employees may not give me the benefit of the doubt, but other people should."

Muslim people are far more likely to be the victims of prejudice now than before the terrorist attacks. The overwhelming majority of Muslim people in North America are generous, compassionate, and are no threat to anyone. The Christian community needs to work against prejudice–in our hearts and in our society. Reaching out may cause us to be misunderstood, but we should still do so.

The page opposite the beginning of this chapter has counsel for keeping safe in thunderstorms. Some parts of North America experience earthquakes; some are frequented by tornadoes; coastal areas can be damaged by hurricanes. All parts of the continent endure thunderstorms.

We anticipate thunderstorms as a part of the natural world. We take precautions, but we don't stop going outside because of them. We learn what we need to do in order to be safe, and we accept occasional thunderstorms as a part of life. Likewise, we need to anticipate some problems in relationships with others, but we should not let those stop us from building new relationships.

Our own strength and our own insight, however, are not sufficient to draw us into lives of greater hospitality and compassion. The person who wants to show Christ-like hospitality and compassion must seek to develop the spiritual life so that Christ's love and strength are continually available. True hospitality is only possible for a life which is grounded in prayer and intimately connected with God. Prayer can transform the way we feel about ourselves, the confidence with which we relate to others, and the fundamental way in which we view the world around us.

This does not mean that we postpone the practice of hospitality until we have reached a certain level in the development of the spiritual life. It does mean that we seek to develop the spiritual life at the same time as we seek to practice greater hospitality. Christ continually blesses us through the people around us and through our lives of prayer.

Prayer and Hospitality

According to Gallup polls and other surveys, most people in North America pray. That includes many people who are disillusioned with organized religion but who still feel a connection with God. Some people pray frequently throughout the day; some pray occasionally; and some pray primarily when faced with a particular problem or dilemma.

Following the events of September 11, 2001, enormous numbers of people turned to prayer as a means of dealing with their fear and their loss. The Reverend Jesse Jackson spoke at a high school in Alexandria, Virginia, and had people hold hands and call out prayers for each other and for peace. Many schools have had spontaneous or planned religious services and times of prayer.

Churches, synagogues, and mosques all over North America and even around the world held special prayer services for the victims of terrorism and for peace. A minister in western Ohio remarked: "We had a community prayer service with people from many different religious traditions taking part. Ecumenical services in recent years have only drawn a handful of people; this service packed our town's largest building."

Hanna Rosin reported in the September 29, 2001, *Washington Post* that in the days following the crisis: "Counselors working in New York and Washington say they were surprised to find once-secular clients confessing a need to pray." As people had difficulty sleeping, concentrating, and overcoming depression, prayer became for many a natural response.

Both of us consider ourselves more students than teachers when it comes to prayer. There are limitations on what we or anyone else can effectively teach on this topic. In *Reaching Out*, Henri Nouwen reminds us that:

> *The paradox of prayer is that we have to learn how to pray while we can only receive it as a gift. . . . We cannot plan, organize or manipulate God; but without a careful discipline, we cannot receive him either* [p. 87, p. 89].

Prayer, ultimately, is a gift from God. God continually seeks to deepen connection with each of us, and our efforts at prayer are always received and cherished by God. The bedtime and meal prayers of a small child are just as pleasing to God as the eloquent prayers of a minister or theologian.

With considerable humility, we offer these guidelines for people who want to deepen the life of prayer, especially in relationship to the practice of hospitality and life in a time of fear:

1. Most of us need to pray with greater frequency and regularity if we are to be more fully open to God's guidance in our lives. Changing from a fearful life to a more confident life of hospitality and compassion is not an easy transition. Occasional prayer will not provide the foundation that we need for a different kind of living. We need God's help on a continuing basis, and God's guidance is most likely to come to us in small stages rather than in sweeping revelations.

In his book *In the Name of Jesus*, Nouwen writes:

> *God is a God of the present and reveals to those*
> *who are willing to listen carefully to the moment*
> *in which they live the steps they are to take toward*
> *the future.* [pp.3-4]

While we make major commitments during our lives, the living out of those commitments happens on a daily basis. Our values are most clearly revealed and our habits are most deeply defined by the decisions and actions of each new day.

Most people reading this book lead busy, perhaps almost frantic lives. Many of us do not feel that we have the time for daily devotions. Those who take that time, however, almost always find that the other activities of the day flow more smoothly.

A life of greater prayer can start in very small ways. Consider, for example:

- Starting the day with prayer.

- Saying a prayer before each meal, including a silent prayer when in the presence of school or work colleagues.

- Saying a prayer each time you get behind the wheel of a car or each time you board public transportation.

- Ending the day with prayer.

The prayers can be very short, sometimes only one or two sentences. If you are not currently praying on a daily basis, simply doing one of the above options will change the way you view the world around you and will deepen your connection with God. In a few weeks time, try adding another time for daily prayer to your schedule. Don't be angry with yourself when you fail to do so; simply do better the next time.

One of the Five Pillars of Islam is the expectation that Muslims around the world will stop to pray five times each day. While those prayers are traditionally recited in Arabic while facing Mecca, some Muslims in North America have made adaptations which feel more comfortable to them. The concept of praying five times a day has much in common with some Christian religious orders which have specified times for daily prayer. That doesn't mean that one should only pray at those designated times, but it does set a minimal standard for communication with God.

2. Work toward a life of greater prayer, in which intimacy with God is a part of everything that you do. As you add more times of prayer to your life, you'll become more aware of God's presence and guidance. You'll find yourself drawn into God's love in the midst of your other activities, and you'll begin to see the world in a different way. In *A Testament of Devotion*, Thomas R. Kelly describes another way of living:

> *There is a way of ordering our mental life on more than one level at once. On one level we may be thinking, discussing, seeing, calculating, meeting all the demands of external affairs. But deep within, behind the scenes, at a profounder level, we may also be in prayer and adoration, song and worship, and a gentle receptiveness to divine breathings. The secular world of today values and cultivates only the first level, assured that there is where the real business of humankind is done. . . . But in a deeply religious culture [people] know that the deep level of prayer and of divine attendance is the most important thing in the world. It is at this deep level that the real business of life is determined.* [p. 27]

When we are immersed in the love of God, we will begin to see people differently. Kelly referred to this as "a tendering of the soul, toward *everything* in creation" [p.35]. As we begin to recognize the presence of Christ in each person we encounter, we will find ourselves loving others more, judging them less, and not very often feeling fearful of them. Some people we may have been inclined to ignore in the past begin to become more important to us. We may also find ourselves less willing to make unworthy compromises for the sake of approval by those whose values are not consistent with our understanding of God's will.

By God's grace and with a commitment to change on our own part, we may find ourselves sharing short prayers for guidance in the midst of our daily activities:

- A prayer before making a decision at home, at work, or in another setting.

- A prayer before meeting someone for the first time.

- A prayer of thanksgiving for a new individual met by phone, by e-mail, or in person.

- A prayer for forgiveness when we have spoken in haste or in anger.

- A prayer for God's help to another person, even to those we see but do not actually know.

- A prayer for God's guidance during a meeting or conference.

- A prayer of thanksgiving in the midst of the day for those we love.

- A prayer of thanksgiving for a blessing we receive.

- A prayer for God's consolation when we are disappointed by others.

At first, we may be very conscious of those short prayers throughout the day. Over the course of time, those prayers can become as natural to us as breathing. *A Testament of Devotion* tells us that it is possible to live a life that is fully immersed in prayer and in direct connection with God.

3. As we gain confidence in the life of prayer, we can deepen our faith by risking prayers for greater openness to

God's guidance. In her marvelous book *A Christian View of Hospitality–Expecting Surprises*, Michele Hershberger writes:

> I decided to pray every morning for God to send
> me a hospitality opportunity, a person I could host,
> a person who would be Jesus to me.   [p. 13]

Such a prayer is a brave one, because God will respond. When we are truly open for new opportunities to interact with others and to do God's will, God will guide us in that process. This is the kind of prayer that has the power to transform our lives. We can pray it with confidence as we gain trust in Christ's guidance and protection of our lives.

Some Prayers for Deeper Intimacy with God and Others

The best prayers are often the prayers of our own hearts, and sometimes they consist of an opening of ourselves to God rather than any verbal expression. In the development of the spiritual life, however, the prayers which have been written by others can play an important role. Worrying too much about how to express ourselves to God can be a barrier to intimacy. The prayers others have found helpful may enable us to express our own desires and hopes. Some prayers have been found so meaningful by so many people that they have been passed down through the centuries.

In this section, we offer a few prayers which may be helpful as you seek to deepen the connection between prayer and hospitality. Some of these prayers do not deal directly with our interactions with other people but deal rather with an overall attitude of openness to God's guidance and protection. That attitude inevitably leads to hospitality and away from fear.

Prayers at the Start of the Day

Rejoice in the Lord always; again I will say, Rejoice. Let your gentleness be known to everyone. The Lord is near. So do not worry about anything, but in everything by prayer and supplication with thanksgiving let your requests be made known to God. And the peace of God, which surpasses all understanding, will guard your hearts and your minds in Christ Jesus. Amen. [Philippians 4:4-7]

My dear Lord, who hast made my soul Thy dwelling place and will never leave me, I ask Thee to rule me, govern me, enclose me, and make me one with Thee in perfect charity. Amen. [Juliana of Norwich]

I pray that, according to the riches of his glory, he may grant that you may be strengthened in your inner being with power through his Spirit, and that Christ may dwell in your hearts through faith, as you are being rooted and grounded in love. I pray that you may have the power to comprehend, with all the saints, what is the breadth and length and height and depth, and to know the love of Christ that surpasses knowledge, so that you may be filled with all the fullness of God. Now to him who by the power at work within us is able to accomplish abundantly far more than all we can ask or imagine, to him be glory in the church and in Christ Jesus to all generations, forever and ever. Amen. [Ephesians 3:16-21]

O God, Who art the unsearchable abyss of peace, the ineffable sea of love, the foundation of blessings, and the bestower of affection, Who sendest peace to those that receive it, open to us this day the sea of Thy love, and water us with the plenteous streams from the riches of Thy grace. Make us children of quietness, and heirs of peace. Enkindle in us the fire of Thy love; sow in us Thy fear; strengthen our weakness by Thy power; bind us closely to Thee and to each other in one firm bond of unity; for the sake of Jesus Christ. Amen. [Syrian Clementine Liturgy]

Lord,
*   make me an instrument of your peace.*
Where there is hatred, let me sow love;
*   where there is injury, pardon;*
*   where there is doubt, faith;*
*   where there is despair, hope;*

where there is darkness, light;
where there is sadness, joy.
O divine Master,
grant that I may not so much seek
to be consoled, as to console;
to be understood, as to understand;
to be loved, as to love.
For it is in giving that we receive;
it is in pardoning that we are pardoned;
it is in dying that we are born to eternal life. Amen.
[St. Francis of Assisi]

O God, I give you deep thanksgiving for the gift of this new day and for all the blessings which will be contained in it. Grant me a discerning heart that I may truly recognize your presence in all those with whom I come in contact this day. Help me, Lord, to be your presence to others; and enable me to receive the gift of your presence from those around me. Forgive me for my sins and for my continuing tendency toward self-centeredness. Keep me open to your guidance and help in the midst of the opportunities, problems, joys, and sorrows which this day may bring. When anger, greed, jealousy, or frustration make it hard for me to recognize your presence in others, clarify my vision and deepen my love. Amen.
[Steve and Fred]

Prayers at the End of the Day

I know, O Lord, and do with all humility acknowledge myself an object altogether unworthy of Thy love; but sure I am, Thou art an object altogether worthy of mine. I am not good enough to serve Thee, but Thou hast a right to the best service I can pay. Do Thou then impart to me some of that excellence, and that shall supply my own want of worth. Help me to cease from sin according to Thy will, that I may be capable of doing Thee service according to my duty. Enable me so to guard and govern myself, so to begin and finish my course, that, when the race of life is run, I may sleep in peace, and rest in Thee. Be with me unto the end, that my sleep may be rest indeed, my rest perfect security, and that security a blessed eternity. Amen. [Augustine]

Remember, O Lord, this city wherein we dwell and every other city and country, and all the faithful who dwell in them. Remember, O Lord, all who travel by land or water, all that labour under sickness or slavery; remember them for health and safety. Remember, O

Lord, those in Thy Holy Church who bring for her good fruit, are rich in good works and forget not the poor. Grant unto us all Thy mercy and loving-kindness, and grant that we may with one mouth and one heart praise and glorify Thy great and glorious name, Father, Son, and Holy Ghost, now, henceforth, and forever. Amen. [Chrysostom]

Thank you, Lord, for the many gifts you have given me. Thank you for your presence in those with whom I have shared the events of this day. Forgive me for those times when I failed to recognize your presence in others or when I was tempted to put my own desires ahead of your will. Gently guide me, Lord, as I seek to more fully desire what you desire and to more fully see others through your great love. Help me overcome the fears which separate me from others and from the best in myself. Grant me a safe night's rest, and be with me in the events of the new day. Fill me with your love, and guide me in sharing that love with others. Amen. [Steve and Fred]

Prayers during the Day

Lord Jesus Christ, have mercy upon me. [The Jesus Prayer]

Help me, Lord, not to be weary of doing little things for your great love. Thank you for regarding not the greatness of the work, but the love with which it is performed. Amen. [Brother Lawrence]

Intensify Thy leadings and drawings in our hearts until their clarity cannot be mistaken, and incline our wills toward them. Lay on us afresh the brothering of the souls of those about us and give us the patience to persist. Kindle in us such a longing for Thee that it will illuminate and blaze through all that we do. Amen. [Thomas R. Kelly]

Prayers for God's Guidance

Gracious Holy Spirit, so much of my life seems to revolve around my interests and my welfare. I would like to live just one day in which everything I did benefited someone besides myself. Perhaps prayer for others is a starting point. Help me to do so without any need for praise or reward. In Jesus' name. Amen. [Richard J. Foster in *Prayer–Finding the Heart's True Home*, p. 201]

O Lord, our Saviour, who hast warned us that thou wilt require much of those to whom much is given; grant that we whose lot is cast in so goodly a heritage may strive together the more abundantly to extend to others what we so richly enjoy; and as we have entered into the labours of other people, so to labour that in their turn others may enter into ours, to the fulfillment of Thy holy will; through Jesus Christ our Lord. Amen. [Augustine]

Eternal source of love and forgiveness, direct us to have the spiritual insight to know that those who try to harm us are in need of our forgiveness and mercy. May we realize that the way to destroy a personal enemy is by overcoming evil with good, by praying for those who persecute us. Amen. [George Fox, founder of the Society of Friends]

My Father, if it is possible, let this cup pass from me; yet not what I want but what you want. Amen. [Matthew 26:39–the prayer of our Lord at Gethsemane]

Lord, I am conscious of living so much of my life governed by fear. I fear failure, I fear rejection by others, I fear being taken advantage of, I fear sickness, I fear lost opportunities, I fear change, I fear death. I fear that I or those I love will be victims of terrorism. Surround me with your great love, and help me put aside my fears. Let me have no fears except those which are appropriate for protection and safety and the doing of your will. Deepen in me a spirit of compassion and hospitality toward others. Grant me this day an opportunity to practice hospitality to another, to be your presence to someone in need. And make me ready, Lord, to receive the blessings you are ready to give me through others. Amen. [Steve and Fred]

Prayers from the Psalms for Protection and Guidance

Even though I walk through the darkest valley,
I fear no evil; for you are with me;
your rod and your staff–they comfort me.
You prepare a table before me in the presence of my enemies;
you anoint my head with oil; my cup overflows.
Surely goodness and mercy shall follow me all the days of my life,
and I shall dwell in the house of the LORD
my whole life long. [Psalm 23:4-6]

As a deer longs for flowing streams,
so my soul longs for you, O God. . . .
Why are you cast down, O my soul,
and why are you disquieted within me?
Hope in God; for I shall again praise him,
my help and my God. [Psalm 42:1, 11]

Create in me a clean heart, O God,
and put a new and right spirit within me. [Psalm 51:10]

O my strength, I will watch for you;
for you, O God, are my fortress. [Psalm 59:9]

Hear my cry, O God; listen to my prayer.
From the end of the earth I call to you,
when my heart is faint.
Lead me to the rock that is higher than I;
for you are my refuge,
a strong tower against the enemy. [Psalm 61:1-3]

For God alone my soul waits in silence;
from him comes my salvation.
He alone is my rock and my salvation,
my fortress; I shall never be shaken. [Psalm 62:2]

For a day in your courts is better than a thousand elsewhere.
I would rather be a doorkeeper in the house of my God
than live in the tents of wickedness.
For the LORD God is a sun and shield; he bestows favor and honor.
No good thing does the LORD withhold
from those who walk uprightly.
O LORD of hosts,
happy is everyone who trusts in you. [Psalm 84:10-12]

You who live in the shelter of the Most High,
who abide in the shadow of the Almighty,
will say to the LORD, "My refuge and my fortress;
my God, in whom I trust."
For he will deliver you from the snare of the fowler
and from the deadly pestilence;
he will cover you with his pinions,
and under his wings you will find refuge;
his faithfulness is a shield and buckler.
You will not fear the terror of the night,

or the arrow that flies by day,
or the pestilence that stalks in darkness,
or the destruction that wastes at noonday. [Psalm 91:1-6]

Where can I go from your spirit?
Or where can I flee from your presence?
If I ascend to heaven, you are there;
if I make my bed in Sheol, you are there.
If I take the wings of the morning
and settle at the farthest limits of the sea,
even there your hand shall lead me,
and your right hand shall hold mine fast.
If I say, "Surely the darkness shall cover me.
and the light around me become night,"
even the darkness is not dark to you;
the night is as bright as the day,
for darkness is as light to you. [Psalm 139:7-12]

Children and Guns

- Children should be taught that if they encounter a gun, they should SALT:
    - Immediately **S**TOP whatever they are doing.
    - **A**VOID touching the gun.
    - **L**EAVE the area at once.
    - **T**ALK to an adult about the gun.

- Hiding a gun is not enough to make children safe. Children can go through all the drawers and cabinets in a house. Even very young children climb on furniture, ladders, or stepping stools to explore high shelves. The best child-proofing methods are the same ones that keep unauthorized adults from gun access OR not having a gun at all.

- Many locking cases for guns have three wheels with numbers on the locking mechanism. It takes an average of only ten minutes to open those locks by systematically trying every combination.

- Children need to be told about the danger of playing with guns. They also need to know the difference between violence in the media and real-life violence.

- Guns and ammunition should be stored separately and locked. Unloaded firearms should also be provided with a gun lock, alarm, or another device to prevent tampering and to make the gun inoperable. Gun storage keys should never be kept in the same location as other keys.

- Do you really need a gun?

Chapter Six:
Hospitality and the Family

Concept: Hospitality has the power to transform how we view our spouses, parents, children, and the others who constitute family. We need to develop appreciation for the changing nature of the family in our time.

"What just amazes me," Carolyn said to her pastor, "is that our daughter went from 125 pounds to 84 pounds before we recognized that something was wrong. Jill had always been so healthy. She ate right. She took part in sports. She did well in school. We just didn't worry about her as much as we did about her older sister or her younger brother.

"She picked up the pace of her physical fitness work, and we were a little concerned about her overdoing it, but we didn't want to pour cold water on her enthusiasm. What should have tipped us off earlier was when she became so picky about what and how much she would eat. It became difficult to cook anything she would eat that the rest of the family would like. When she suggested that she just start fixing her own meals, I was actually a little relieved. I wondered in the back of my mind if she had some kind of eating disorder, but that was something that would happen to someone else's child, not to ours.

"We saw that she had lost quite a bit of weight, and sometimes that worried us. But most of this happened during the fall and the winter, so we weren't seeing her in sleeveless blouses or shorts and didn't realize just how emaciated she had become. We'd try talking to her about her looking too thin, but she got very defensive. We thought that, after all, she was sixteen years old, so there was a limit on how much we should be trying to control her.

"Then one day early in the spring, she came downstairs wearing shorts and a tank top to go for a run. Her arms and legs looked like sticks to me. I told her that we had to go into the bathroom and use the scales to see how much she weighed. She started crying, and I had to physically drag her to the scales. She got on them, and she was at 84 pounds, including the weight of her clothes and running shoes.

"We went straight to our family doctor's office. I don't know if I will ever be able to forgive myself for not recognizing what was happening sooner. I guess I just didn't want to deal with it until it was so clear there was no choice at all. And then I wonder what my husband and I did that caused her to develop the eating disorder. Where did we go wrong?"

Keith did not know Carolyn, but he certainly could identify with not having faced a problem as early as he should have. Keith came home from work on a Friday evening to find his wife's closet empty and a note taped to the beer in the refrigerator:

> *Keith, I'm sorry to do it this way, but you just don't hear me when I try talking to you. Being married to you feels like being in prison. I know you mean well and think you're protecting me, but what you're doing is controlling me. I earn as much money as you, but you make all the financial decisions. If you feel like sex, we have it whether I feel like it or not. You decide where we go for Thanksgiving and Christmas. My family always has to take second place. It's gone on for nine years, and I can't handle it any longer. You pushed it over the edge two nights ago when you said that it was time for us to have a child. I've been wanting to do that for two years, but you wouldn't have it. Now that you're ready, you expect me to rearrange my life and my career so we can do it. Keith, I'm sorry, but I realized that I don't want you to be the father of a child of mine. I love you, but I can't live with you.*
> *Becky*

We may live with increased fear of terrorist attacks, but problems within the family can be even more devastating than any suffering caused by outside forces. We do not want our anxiety about the danger of plane crashes, bombs, or biological weapons to prevent us from recognizing the needs of those with whom we most intimately share our lives. While there are limitations on how much any of us as individuals can do to protect ourselves against terrorism, there are many things we can do to lower the probability of broken relationships with those we love. The deepening of those relationships enriches our lives and strengthens us to better deal with external threats.

The practice of hospitality certainly involves reaching out to strangers and to persons we do not know well, but it also impacts how we relate to those who are the closest to us. True hospitality means that we recognize the presence of Christ in those with whom we share our lives. And hospitality has nothing to do with ownership or control. Hospitality means recognizing that the other persons in our lives are guests and that those relationships are gifts from God to be cherished. For most of us, the practice of hospitality has some important implications for our relationships with family and close friends.

Hospitality and Our Children

Carolyn suffered from deep guilt for not having more quickly recognized the seriousness of her daughter's eating disorder. With perfect hindsight, she can recognize the signs that should have motivated action from herself or her husband. Parents all over North America have had similar experiences in missing the early warning signs not only of eating disorders but also of drugs, alcohol, sexual abuse, and violence. It's easy to fall into the trap of ignoring or rationalizing away events linked to problems that are painful to face. Hospitality is not a cure for Carolyn's dilemma, but a life focused on hospitality does have some implications for parenting.

1. Hospitality recognizes that children are gifts from God, not properties to rule over. This in no way means that children should not be disciplined and taught to behave. Recognizing our children as gifts from God carries with it the responsibility to raise them with the values, beliefs, and habits that are appropriate for all the sons and daughters of God.

The focus of our decision-making in raising our children should be on what is best for them rather than on what is best for ourselves. In our fast-paced society with what seem like ever-increasing demands in the workplace, it's easy for us to begin seeing our children as an inconvenience. Tired from the work and stress of the day, we can all too easily be tempted to take the easy way when dealing with our children. Many parents come home from work needing to relax and unwind, and they understandably do not want "one more thing" to deal with or handle.

The needs and problems of our children, however, are not just "one more thing" to handle or one more problem to solve. Our children are gifts from God, entrusted to our care. There is nothing that those of us who are parents do which is of any greater importance than taking the time to make the right decisions concerning our children. That can at times mean confronting them about concerns over drugs, alcohol, weight, sex, or violence.

Bill visited with a group in his church about the pace of life in his family. He said, "What really got me was when our son asked if we would help him buy a motorcycle. The first thing I thought of was, 'If he gets a cycle, then we won't have to drive him places anymore.' I felt this relief wash over me, and I started to say, 'Sure, we'll help you get one.' Then I realized that I was thinking of my convenience and my wife's convenience. I wasn't evaluating whether or not a motorcycle was a good thing for him to own at his age or whether or not it was good for us to help him buy one.

"I also wasn't thinking about all the conversations that we have with him when we drive him to practices and meetings and games. I know all that has to end sometime, but is this the time that it should? Maybe we have one more valuable year of being his transportation. Anyway, the decision shouldn't be about what is easiest for us."

2. Seeing our children as guests reminds us that we are not responsible for everything they do. Our children are far more than extensions of us. They are not going to handle every situation in the way that we wish they would. No matter how hard we try, we are not going to protect them from every problem which life brings. Henri Nouwen, in *Reaching Out*, provides this perspective:

> *The awareness that children are guests can be a liberating awareness because many parents suffer from deep guilt feelings toward their children, thinking that they are responsible for everything their sons or daughters do* [p. 57].

Those are words of comfort for parents like Carolyn who find themselves obsessed with the question: "Where did we go wrong?" There's not always a clear answer to that question. Eating disorders, drugs, alcohol, early sexual activity, school problems, social problems, financial hardship, depression, suicide, violence, and other difficulties that afflict our children usually have multiple causes.

Parents can place too much responsibility on themselves for what happens to their children and for what their children do. Hospitality recognizes that children are guests in our lives, that they have their own identity and values, and that we cannot and should not attempt to control everything they do. Recognizing that we want them to mature into the people God has created them to be should free us to increasingly let go of our efforts to control as they move through adolescence.

"The problem for most of us," Carol, a child psychologist, said to a parenting class at her church, "is that we don't do enough to influence the behavior of our children when they are small and then we try to regain control when they become teenagers. That never works. If you're going to use the word control, then the time to exercise control is when children are young. When we attempt to increase our control over their behavior after they hit the teen years, we are going against the normal developmental tasks of that age, which are focused on their taking increasing responsibility for their own decisions and gradually breaking free of our authority."

3. Practicing hospitality with our children means doing our best and then trusting the result to God, who is the parent of us all. We do not achieve perfection in parenting or in any other area of life. Some mistakes are inevitable, but God can and does help us and our children. Susan, a single parent, talked to her mother about her feelings on parenting. "I felt like such a failure when Angie was having so much trouble as a child. The divorce was hard on Angie and David, but David didn't seem as badly affected at the time. David was thirteen, and Angie was seven when we separated. David seemed to just move ahead as the perfect child, trying to take care of Angie and of me.

"Angie had such serious problems. She couldn't sleep at night. She pulled her hair and picked at her skin during the day. She didn't deal well with living with me during the week and with her father on the weekends. As I look back, I realize that I neglected David a lot of the time because Angie was so demanding. How could I ignore problems that severe?

"But Angie came through those years and has turned out fine. She has such a healthy self-confidence as a college student that it's hard to believe she had so many problems as a child. David is the one I feel badly about now. He's doing all right with his life, but he's told me a couple of times how much he hated his sister those years right after the divorce and how angry he was with his father and with me for giving all the attention to Angie. He felt neglected, and he was right. He just always seemed to be doing well, and that's what we wanted to believe."

"But what else could you have done?" her mother asked. "You certainly couldn't ignore Angie's problems. You only had so many hours in the day, and you had to work and earn a living. Your ex-husband was in the same spot. You made the best decisions you could at the time. Sure, you can look back now and see that more should have been done for David. But where would you have found the time to do it? David may carry some anger, and you need to let him talk about it. David, however, has turned into a fine young adult, and he's having a good life. Both of your children turned out well."

"Perhaps I wouldn't feel this way," Susan acknowledged, "if we'd never gotten the divorce. I've always assumed that Angie's problems came about because of the divorce."

"Maybe they did. But there could have been a different set of problems if you'd stayed married to each other as angry as the two of you had become. You have to recognize that you did the best job you knew how to do. It wasn't perfect, but God doesn't expect perfection of us. You need to cut yourself some slack and be thankful that your children both turned out so well."

Susan's dilemma is one which many parents experience as we live in a time when two out of three children in the United States will spend at least part of their childhood in a single parent home. The nature of family life has changed. We may not feel good about some of those changes, but they are a fact of life. Raising a child is difficult for a husband and wife together, and it is even more challenging for a single parent.

The truth is that, as parents, we don't do everything right. The marriage decisions that we made or didn't make before having children weren't always the right ones, and there are consequences that flow from that as well. What we are called to do is our best. We must trust the results to God.

4. Hospitality does mean taking seriously our responsibility for the children God has entrusted to our care. The page opposite the beginning of this chapter provides thoughts on *Children and Guns*. It is very difficult to have a gun in the house and to be absolutely certain that children will not gain access to it. A police officer kept her service revolver in a case which had three wheels with numbers on the locking mechanism. She had the code set to 7, 7, 7 because she thought that would make it easy for her to access the gun in an emergency. She felt confident that the locking mechanism was adequate to protect her children.

While clearing the table one evening with her husband, they heard their two children giggling loudly from the master bedroom. They weren't alarmed, but they did wonder what the children had gotten into. They walked into the bedroom and discovered their five-year-old son aiming the service revolver at their three-year-old daughter. The children were both giggling as the big brother said, "Raise your hands, or I'll shoot!" The gun was loaded.

Children are incredibly creative–and at times downright crafty. Their son proudly told them that it had taken him only a few tries to get into the gun case. He knew that the security code on their household burglar alarm system was 3, 3, 3 so he figured the numbers on the gun case would also be a single number repeated.

Police officers have guns. Clearly that particular officer needed a new solution for storing the gun while at home. But how many of the rest of us really need to have weapons? For most of us, the probability of needing a weapon in self-defense is much smaller than the probability of the weapon being used to injure or kill someone we love.

Hospitality means not being governed by our fears in the community–or in our homes. Anxiety about the need for self-defense may cause us to introduce a danger into our homes which is as great as that of any terrorist or criminal. We want to protect our children, but that at times may mean protecting them from our own fears.

The fact that children are guests in our homes should free us from unhealthy guilt over all that they do; but far from absolving us from responsibility for protecting them, it increases the magnitude of that responsibility. These are the children of God, entrusted to us. We do not protect well when anxiety dominates our thinking.

Many of us are aware that the events of September 11, 2001 carry the danger of causing children to grow up in fear. The televised images of airplanes hitting the World Trade Center towers formed strong impressions on the minds of people of all ages but especially children. For some very young children, each repeated viewing of those frightening scenes represents a new incident. Certainly we should control the amount of television that young children watch, but we should also remember that they are continually learning from our words and actions as adults.

- What are children taught by the importance we place on having a gun in the home?

- What are children taught if we are reluctant to go to shopping malls because of terrorist concerns?

- What are children taught if we talk about the danger of anthrax or other disease each time we open the mail?

- What are children taught if we make unfavorable comments about people of Middle Eastern appearance or names?

- What are children taught if we speak disparagingly of the Muslim faith?

- What are children taught if we make comments about wanting people in other countries killed?

And fear can affect our thinking in more ways than having firearms too readily accessible. Many of our children and grand-children lead lives which are frantic as they participate in every possible school and community activity. It's no wonder that people like Bill are relieved when it's possible for children to start transporting themselves to activities and events.

But there is a possibility that our lives have become too frantic, that both we and our children are attempting to do too many different things. In our desire to see that our children have every experience possible, we may be overloading them and ourselves. We fear depriving our children of important opportunities or making ourselves appear "different" from others by not participating in the same activities, but the frantic pace which results may be depriving our children of other needful experiences. The quality of family life inevitably suffers when its members are pulled in too many different directions.

Those of us who are involved in churches need to be careful that the multitude of church activities we participate in do not further pull our families in multiple directions. Most of the time, however, the church comes in second place to the demands of school activities, athletic events, and other opportunities. Missing a swimming or hockey or music practice can put a child off the team; missing a church youth group meeting does not carry similar consequences.

What do we really want to have happen in the lives of our children? How busy is too busy? How can meaningful family time be protected? What priorities do we teach our children by the decisions we make with them? These are all serious questions as we think about our responsibility to the guests in our homes.

Spouses and Significant Others

In a meeting with parents of teenagers, Steve asked the group what they felt their children needed to be taught to prepare them for dating experiences and marriage. One parent said, "By all means, teach them to put their marriage partner first, not last. My husband and I are continually giving each other the leftovers. We put our work first and then some of our other obligations. We share with each other the time and emotional energy that remains when everything else has been done. That's no way to nurture a relationship with the person you love more than anyone else in the world."

It sure isn't. The trap she described, though, is one which snares many couples. We are busy. We are often under stress. There are work demands and community demands and parenting demands and (for many of those reading this book) church demands. It's easy to have little time, energy, or patience left for one's spouse or significant other. What does hospitality say about the way we interact with our most important partners in life?

1. Hospitality means that we see the spouse as a cherished gift of God, not as a person to be controlled. Control issues were at the root of the problems Keith and Becky had, as described in the beginning of this chapter. Keith in fact did not recognize just how controlling he had become of Becky and of their relationship. Unable to successfully communicate with him about it, she finally left.

Our expectations of marriage are sometimes unrealistic. It's not at all unusual for a person to get married with the anticipation that his or her partner will change over the course of the relationship in certain desirable ways. Life continually involves change, of course, but it's very unrealistic to expect that another person can be molded into the image we desire. Our efforts to change each other in intimate relationships become efforts to control, and those efforts are resented even when they are successful.

It's easy to convince ourselves that our desires to change a spouse are rooted in wanting what is best for the spouse and for our relationship. That may indeed be our intention. But the result is rarely positive. People do not want to be shaped by someone else. Hospitality teaches us to cherish rather than to control and to work openly on mutual change rather than inflicting our will on the other person.

2. Hospitality means sharing equally in decisions about money, sex, children, and other vital areas of life together. Recognizing the other person as a gift from God, with whom we have the opportunity to share a lifetime, means more than an absence of control. It means working together positively to shape the kind of relationship which will be most meaningful.

Couples who believe in hospitality, who recognize the presence of Christ in each other, are not going to be concerned about which person earns the most money. They are going to be concerned about making mutual decisions concerning the use of the material resources that they have.

Becky and Keith had fallen into the trap of Keith making all the decisions concerning their sexual relationship. If he was in the mood, something happened. If he was not in the mood, nothing happened. Becky had to feel like an object that was owned rather than a person who was cherished.

Decisions about children also need to be made together, recognizing Christ's presence in each other and in the children God has given. When children are young, one parent, who is able to spend more time at home, may appropriately carry a larger share of the nurturing function. That does not mean that the other parent should be excluded from major decisions affecting the lives of their children, and it certainly does not exempt the other parent from the responsibility of being involved in the lives of their children.

In all these areas and others, viewing one's spouse as a person to cherish means a continual desire to share in major decisions. That's part of the joy of life together.

3. Hospitality means treating one's partner BETTER than anyone else, not worse. The decision to marry another person and the decision to have children are two of the most important relationship decisions which we can make. Those are the relationships which should receive our greatest energy, our greatest commitment, and our greatest patience. One's husband or wife should not receive our emotional leftovers.

That doesn't mean it's always easy to put the other person first, especially during times of high stress at work. Obviously the best intentioned and most sincere of us will make some mistakes in this area, and it's important to readily extend understanding and forgiveness to each other. But if one recognizes that a spouse is continually receiving or giving emotional leftovers, then it's time for a careful look at where time and emotional energy are going.

4. And those who are reading these words and are single should remember that being single does not mean being incomplete. As wonderful as marriage can be, that isn't the right fit for everyone. Not all people are called to be married, and not all people will thrive in a marriage environment. Much of what has been shared in this chapter will still apply to those who choose to have long term relationships with significant others to whom they are not married. The practice of hospitality should apply to all relationships.

Parents and Grandparents

We can all celebrate the fact that people are living longer than ever, and that trend appears likely to continue. Changes in lifestyle and advances in medical technology have made it possible for many of us to live longer, healthier, and more vibrant lives than were possible for earlier generations.

With these improvements in life quality and life expectancy, however, have come some increased concerns about how to relate to elderly parents and grandparents. Adult children, already under pressure from work, from home, and from community responsibility, may find it difficult to relate as positively as they want to their own parents and grandparents. The matter is further complicated by the fact that some people live hundreds or even thousands of miles from their parents or grandparents.

Again, we need to think about these relationships from the perspective of hospitality. Our parents and grandparents are truly gifts from God, without whose love we would not ourselves exist. Certainly there are not any perfect parent-child relationships, and our relationships with our parents and grandparents can sometimes be clouded by unresolved issues. That reality, however, should not be permitted to blind us to the presence of Christ in them and to the very special relationship which their lives have to our lives.

Fran attended a spiritual life workshop. During the course of that workshop, she identified one of her chief spiritual burdens as her failure to do as much as she should for her parents, who lived 500 miles away. She had a brother who lived ten miles from them, and it had become easy to depend on him for offering help to their parents when needed. As she prayed in a silent time in the workshop, Fran realized that her parents did not particularly need her help, they needed her. And she still needed them. The lack of connection with them filled her with guilt and even affected her relationship with her husband and with her own children. She at times found herself resenting having moved so far from her parents because of her husband's employment and not being able to visit them more often because of the vacation plans made as a family.

She resolved that it was time to make some changes. She wrote down four resolutions at the workshop:

1. To start calling her parents once a week, every week. If her husband and children were home and could be part of the conversation, fine. But she was no longer going to avoid making the call because others were not there to share in it.

2. To involve her husband and children in more advance planning for holidays and vacation time, so that the need to see her parents wasn't continually squeezed out by last minute decisions.

3. To make at least one trip a year by herself to visit with her parents in addition to whatever traveling she did there with her husband and children.

4. To start writing a letter once a week to her parents. They loved getting written communications, and it would only take her a few minutes to do it.

As she started acting on those resolutions, she felt a significant burden lifting from her shoulders and felt her life being enriched by the deepened connection with her parents. They were overjoyed by the change. And the fact that Fran started viewing contact with her parents as important began to cause her husband and children to view it as important as well. They learned to cherish her parents, and their own lives were enriched.

The Home as a Place of Hospitality

As Steve grew up, the dining room table in his family's home was the site of many significant activities. The dining room itself was located in the center of the house. One passed through the dining room to get from the front of the house to the kitchen and family area or to get from the back of the house to the living room.

The oak table was circular and had first belonged to Steve's great-grandparents. It had been in his mother's home throughout her childhood and then had been a gift from her parents. When Steve (an only child), his mother, and his father ate at home, they sat at that table. They shared prayer before each meal, and they sometimes had devotions at the table after supper.

The table was also where his mother, a teacher, graded papers during the evening and where Steve often did his homework. Though his father more often used a desk for his work at home, he would occasionally join Steve and his mother at the table. His father, who liked practical jokes, would sometimes deliberately cover the papers of his wife and Steve with his own work and not reveal what he had done until they had searched in vain for their materials.

When there were family decisions to be made, the three of them sat together at that table. Steve's decisions on church membership, vocation, and college and graduate school selection were all made at that table. His parents decided there when to buy and sell their small businesses (a restaurant, a tavern, and a movie theater) and when to retire. Steve remembers meaningful conversations with his parents when people they knew died or experienced great tragedy in their lives. He also remembers times when his father, who was a township supervisor and thus responsible for financial assistance to many people, sat at that table to talk with those who were experiencing difficulty in their lives.

They often entertained, and it was easy for a couple of other persons to join them at the table. His father sometimes invited transients who came to him for financial assistance to join the family for a meal, and Steve's life was enriched through the discussions with those persons. For larger groups, there were additional leaves which could be inserted in the table, so that it could comfortably accommodate at least ten people.

Steve's parents are deceased, and the table now sits in an office he maintains in a local church. He continues to work at that table occasionally, and it's also the setting for various meetings. Steve feels certain that his parents would be especially pleased by the conversations of a young adult class which meets around the table each Sunday to talk about the Bible.

There is a sacred quality to that dining room table because of the ways in which it has been used over the years. Steve can still sit at the table and feel a strong sense of connection to his parents and to God.

Many of our homes have places or objects which become symbols of our faith, which are made sacred by the manner in which they are used. For some it may be a dining room table; for others a sofa; for some couples the bedroom is a place of both physical and spiritual intimacy; for others a grill, coffee pot, popcorn popper, or refrigerator door. Some families focus on objects like a Bible, a cross, a candle, or a family cup which take on special significance. Think about such places or objects in your own home. What would they be? How can you use such objects or places as part of the ritual of your home life?

The home is one of the primary settings in our lives for the practice of hospitality. It is the place where we show hospitality not only to those who live together as part of the family but also to those who visit us. If we want to broaden our hospitality, the home setting is a wonderful place for doing so.

The Scriptures remind us of the power which comes from sharing food. Isaiah 25:6 proclaims:

> *On this mountain, the LORD of hosts will make for all*
> *peoples*
> *a feast of rich food, a feast of well-aged wines,*
> *of rich food filled with marrow, of well-aged wines*
> *strained clear.*

The Lord's Supper or Eucharist has roots in the traditional Sabbath evening meal that was common in Jewish homes and in the Passover meal which was celebrated annually. The ordinary substances of bread and wine take on special meaning. Luke 14:13-14 reminds us that Jesus wants us to invite a broad spectrum of guests to the meals we serve:

> *But when you give a banquet, invite the poor,*
> *the crippled, the lame, and the blind. And you*
> *will be blessed, because they cannot repay you,*
> *for you will be repaid at the resurrection of the*
> *righteous.*

Think about these questions:

- How fragmented has your home life become? Could you benefit from a greater effort to eat one meal a day together as a family? Would a weekly devotion at mealtime help the quality of spiritual life in your home?

- How welcome do the friends of your children feel in your home? How could you help them feel more welcome? If you have no children at home, are there children in your neighborhood who would enjoy your hospitality?

- How frequently do you invite other family and friends to share in meals and to visit in your home?

- Have you considered inviting people who are new to your neighborhood or church to come share in meals with you?

- Have you thought about the possibility of sharing your home with an exchange student? With a foster child? With someone recovering from a drug or alcohol problem who needs a place to live? Is it possible that God is calling you to a ministry of such hospitality?

Remember that hospitality does not depend on the affluence reflected in our homes or on the amount of time spent preparing a meal. While we may be self-conscious concerning the quality of our home furnishings or the cleanliness of our rooms, those who visit us form their opinions based on the warmth of our welcome rather than on the physical characteristics of the house. In the busy times in which we are living, an elaborate home-cooked meal, while certainly appreciated, may not always be realistic. We can show hospitality through the sharing of pizza, soup and sandwiches, or carry-out food. Again, it is the warmth of the welcome we show others that determines their response to our hospitality. We should not let too little time and too much pressure keep us from the blessings that come to us as we use the home as a base for hospitality to others.

Children and the Internet

- The Internet is a fantastic resource for people of all ages and offers exciting opportunities for children. Just as you wouldn't let your children be near a busy street without supervision or rules, you need to help them be safe and wise in their use of the Internet.

- Explore the Internet with your child. Learn more about the interests of your child and provide guidance. Go to sites especially developed for children.

- The best tool your child has for being safe on the Internet is his or her mind! Teach children about the presence of pornography, hate literature, and exploitation on the Internet and help them understand why you don't want them exposed to it.

- Use a commercial Internet Service Provider which offers parental controls that can block many kinds of offensive information.

- Continue to monitor your children when they are online. If they start to become uneasy or defensive when you enter the room, that could be a sign they are doing something of which you would not approve.

- Warn them about giving out their name, address, phone, password, or school to people they don't know. Remind them never to agree to meet face-to-face with someone they've met online. They should always talk with you about such requests.

Chapter Seven:
Nurturing Hospitality

Concept: How hospitality can help us reclaim a sense of community in the neighborhoods where we live, in the workplace, with the people with whom we do business, and with some persons we may encounter only once.

Fred, his wife Joice, and three members of their family made a trip by car from Ohio to Alaska. As they crossed into Canada, customs officials asked Fred, who was driving their vehicle, if they had any firearms, mace, or pepper spray. Fred replied that they did not. Then he was asked more specifically about rifles, shotguns, or handguns. When he responded negatively to those questions, he was asked if they had any weapons at home. Fred said that they did not.

They were asked to pull aside. Then they were asked again about weapons and about their destination. When the women in the group went inside the customs station to use the restroom, they were approached by a female officer who asked, "Don't the men have any firearms? It would be better to tell us." They responded by saying that there were no firearms and that, as a part of their church tradition, they did not believe in violence and chose not to own weapons.

Their vehicle and luggage were searched, and of course no weapons were found. As they worked at repacking the vehicle, Fred asked one of the Canadian officers why there was so much concern about weapons and why they had been searched. He was told, "It's very unusual for us to encounter people from the United States who don't have weapons. They may not have brought them along, but they almost always have them at home. When you said that you had no weapons at home, that made us think you could be lying, so we decided to search your vehicle. You people in the U.S. have such fear that you arm yourselves. That's not allowed in Canada and frightens us." This incident happened prior to September 11, 2001.

The Absence of Hospitality

Of course it's impossible for us to know all the thinking that went into the search of Fred's vehicle by the customs officials. Perhaps people heading for Alaska are considered more likely to be going hunting; perhaps the number and age of the people in the vehicle was a factor. In any event, it is clear that those of us in the United States have cause for concern if we are appearing as fearful to people in other countries as the Canadian authorities indicated to Fred.

The interaction with the customs officials posed an interesting issue of hospitality for Fred and his family. How does a person show hospitality to those who are questioning your integrity and making your life difficult by searching your vehicle? That issue is a much larger one for all of us in North America since the events of September 11, 2001. Airport security and customs inquiries are much more intense and affect everyone who travels by airplane or chooses to cross the border into another country. Suspicion has also increased toward those traveling by train or bus.

Based on our personal experiences since that date and on the stories we have heard from others, discourtesy and rudeness seem to be synonymous with improved security by airport personnel and customs officials. We are not personally convinced that increased security has to mean the complete abandonment of hospitality by officials and travelers. Ordinary, decent people are being treated as potential criminals with an absence of any obligation of basic courtesy and hospitality. Increased searches do not necessitate angry scowls, rude tones of voice, and the absence of "please" or "thank you." Sincere apologies for especially intrusive and inconvenient searches would do much to soften the process but are rarely experienced. Likewise, courtesy by travelers can help the process, if airport and customs officials can learn that hospitality is not a cover for terrorist activity. Rather than reassuring us of our safety as we travel, the current procedures and attitudes contribute to the fearful manner in which we live. It is like giving the terrorists victory over our quality of life.

Fred and his family chose to respond to all the inquiries at the Canadian border with honesty and with courtesy, even when the tone of officials was not particularly courteous toward them.

When they had been cleared of carrying any weapons, it was possible for Fred to ask for further explanation of what had happened and to make a stronger witness to his own beliefs about avoiding both violence and weapons which can be used for violence.

In the process of talking with others about this book, we had several persons talk to us about the lack of hospitality that they had experienced in hospitals. It seems particularly ironic to experience this short-coming in an institution whose name is found in the word hospitality!

People who go to the hospital often are fearful–patients are fearful of what procedures may be inflicted on them and of what those procedures may reveal; friends and family are fearful for the welfare of those they go to visit. Those who manage and work in hospitals are presumably not fearful of the patients, friends, and families who come; but hospital employees are often working under huge amounts of stress and are perhaps governed in part by fear of not doing their jobs right. The result, unfortunately, is sometimes an atmosphere that is not conducive to the healing that hospitals exist to provide. Those of us who work in hospitals or visit them frequently on a professional basis, such as clergy, may start to take the atmosphere for granted. Think about these situations:

- A woman spent six hours in the surgical waiting area, expecting to be informed of what was happening to her husband, who had required immediate surgery because of a tragic automobile accident. Her persistent requests to the staff member on duty were met with the firm reassurance that she would be contacted when something was known. As it turned out, however, her husband had been out of surgery for three hours, during which he had been in the recovery room without her and then taken to a hospital room. She had received no notification from the physicians, nurses, or reception staff. She finally got his room number by calling hospital information from a pay phone in the lobby. Her husband had been very concerned about why she was not with him but had been unable to get anyone to look for her.

127

- A man who was 83 years old was informed by a cardiac surgeon, on the basis of an arteriogram, that he needed to have immediate bypass surgery. The man's overall health was not good, and both he and his wife felt that they needed another opinion before agreeing to such a major surgery. The surgeon was offended by what he took as a lack of confidence on the part of the patient and his wife. In order to leave the hospital and to get another opinion, the patient had to check out "against medical advice." He and his wife felt badly treated not only by the surgeon but also by the nursing staff and the administrative staff of the hospital, all of whom were angry over their not immediately accepting the recommendation. They went to a university-connected medical center for a second opinion. It was the opinion of three specialists there that he should not have bypass surgery. His body was already forming collaterals around the most damaged coronary artery, and he was sufficiently weak from other health complications that he was not a good candidate for the surgery. The man just celebrated his 88th birthday and feels much better than he did at 83.

And of course there are numerous other examples that could be shared. Many people reading this book have had the experience of being made to feel that their insurance coverage and financial health were of greater concern to a hospital upon admission than their physical health.

Hospitals and medical staff who make a concerted effort to be sensitive to the needs of patients and to help patients feel less fearful can create a very different atmosphere. It is often a matter of focus. Those hospitals which see the needs of staff members and the institution as the primary purpose for their existence rarely reflect positive hospitality. Those which are focused on the needs of patients and their families extend a courtesy, a helpfulness, indeed a hospitality which help the healing process and lower the fears of those who enter their doors.

Lack of hospitality, of course, isn't always related to fear. Sometimes the lack of hospitality which we experience is simply based on discourtesy, on being in too big a hurry, or on failing to think about the consequences of our actions. Some of us, who show decent hospitality under ordinary circumstances, display a different personality when we get behind the wheel of an automobile. How often have you seen someone:

- Complaining about other people all driving too slowly and getting in the way?

- Complaining about other people all driving too fast and recklessly?

- Honking the horn when disgusted that someone else is not reacting more quickly to a traffic condition, even though no one is in danger?

- Swearing about someone else's driving?

- Needlessly cutting off someone else?

- Speeding up to make it difficult for another person to merge in front?

- Speeding up to make it hard for someone to pass?

Is it possible that you yourself may have fallen into some of those behavioral traps?

The page opposite the beginning of this chapter shares some guidelines concerning children and the Internet. E-mail and the Internet bring new opportunities to display both courtesy and rudeness to others. The Internet is in many ways an impersonal medium; we often do not know the persons with whom we interact in Chat Rooms or from whom we read messages on Internet bulletin boards or discussion groups. Many people write angry responses to things which irritate them, often sharing statements that they would never make over the telephone or place in a traditional letter.

Some readers of this book will remember the case of Karla Faye Tucker, who was convicted of murder and in February of 1998 became the first woman in many years to be executed. Because of a religious conversion while imprisoned which seemed to truly transform her life, many people, including some within the prison system itself, had attempted to get her life spared by the courts or by the governor. People on both sides of the issue had strong feelings. For two weeks, Steve followed a very hot debate through an Internet bulletin board. Steve was concerned about the fact that the opinions ran about two to one in favor of her execution. Coming from a peace tradition, Steve was not comfortable with capital punishment and especially not in this situation.

When he posted a couple of thoughts of his own about the debate, he discovered that not all of the responses to him went to the bulletin board–some came directly to him by e-mail. Much of that e-mail reflected very strong emotions. For example:

- "She deserves to die and good riddance to her."

- "Rip her arms and legs off, and then chop her into hamburger to feed the other losers on death row."

- "You are a pathetic son of a b---- to have taken her side."

- "You dirty son of a b----. You've probably never lost someone you loved, or you'd be in favor of the murder of everyone like her."

The anonymity of the Internet certainly lowers the inhibitions of people. It's very doubtful that those same people would have written letters to Steve with the same language and even more doubtful that they would have used it in a face-to-face conversation with him.

But those nasty responses do not have Steve soured on the process of online discussion. He sent this response to everyone who referred to him in terms that reflected negatively on his mother:

> *I wonder if any of us think through the way that we use words in the anonymous environment of the Internet and of e-mail to people we don't know. You are probably a good person, but you used some language that is a problem to me. My mother died last year, and it upsets me to have people try to insult me by using language which reflects negatively on her memory. I sincerely hope that was a result of strong emotion and not really a reflection of your character.*

Steve sent those words to fifteen people, and three of them wrote back expressing their regret and thanking him for making them aware of the impact of their words on others.

The practice of hospitality is not helped by the reality that we live not only in a fearful time but also in an annoying time. Everyone reading this book has no doubt had to deal with telemarketing calls during the evening. In a single evening, one of the authors of this book received by phone:

- A "special, limited" offer on siding for their home.

- Two credit card offers.

- One disability insurance offer.

- A college alumni fund-raising call.

- A local charitable institution fund-raising call.

- An offer of a "free" weekend in a hotel in exchange for visiting a new time-share in Florida.

- A call offering a lower mortgage rate from a company which had incorrect information on both name and address.

- Two calls which had no one on the line–almost certainly because they had been automatically dialed and then no sales agent was free when the phone was answered.

It's enough to make you get caller ID. And it's enough to make you feel very uncharitable toward those who call. Telemarketing folks have also come up with an interesting choice of words when the person they want is not home: "There's no message; this is just a courtesy call." A courtesy call that interrupts the evening meal? We don't think so! Certainly those calls reflect an absence of hospitality on the part of those who are phoning, but decisions about how to respond to those calls challenge our understanding of hospitality.

Reclaiming Hospitality

We do not have to be victims of our own fears or of the fears of others. We may not be able to change the attitudes of customs officials, airport security guards, insensitive hospital staff, or telemarketers; but we can modify our own attitudes and behaviors. It's possible for us to reclaim meaningful hospitality in a wide range of relationships with other people, including persons we may not know and may never see again. In this section we offer some specific strategies which may be helpful to you.

Behind the Wheel

1. When getting behind the wheel to drive, offer this prayer or similar words:

> *Keep me safe as I drive, Lord. Help me be alert and careful. Protect me from what I cannot control. Help me, Lord, to be aware of your presence in the other drivers and pedestrians I encounter, especially in those whose actions may be irritating to me. Grant me patience, kindness, and hospitality toward others. Amen.*

2. Remember that speeding or taking other chances rarely makes any significant difference in how long it takes to reach our destinations. Hurrying across a railroad track, speeding through a yellow light, or cutting off someone else, however, can cause an accident, which might permanently keep you from your destination. If you are concerned about being somewhere on time, try leaving a few minutes earlier than usual. That single action will likely help more than all the hurrying behind the wheel of the car that one is tempted to do.

When you get stuck waiting for a train or delayed at a traffic signal, say a short prayer thanking God for the gift of the ability to drive, thanking God for the other people around you, and asking God to grant you patience. Remember that it is very unlikely that a few seconds or even a few minutes lost are going to have that great an impact on your day–unless you convince yourself that they will.

3. The fact that someone else drives like a jerk doesn't mean that you should worsen the situation by also driving like a jerk. Many of us have a reflexive response to negative behavior by others. We respond in kind without thinking about it, but that action in fact makes the environment even less hospitable. Driving an automobile that weighs one-and-a-half or two tons at speeds of thirty, fifty, or seventy miles an hour is not the best time to get into a disagreement. Don't cut off someone who has cut you off. Don't pull over to keep someone who annoys you from passing. Don't speed up to make it difficult for someone to get in front of you.

4. Take the initiative to show hospitality to other drivers and to pedestrians. For example:

- Pull back and create room to make it easier for someone to merge in front of you.

- When two lanes narrow to one, leave room between your car and the car in front sufficient to let others pull in front of you.

- When it's safe to do so in terms of other traffic, grant the right of way to pedestrians, even if they don't have it coming–especially when it's a rainy day or the pedestrian has limited mobility.

- Use your horn only to avoid accidents, not to express your irritation. If you encounter, for example, an elderly person who is driving hesitantly, be courteous rather than blaring your horn and raising his or her anxiety.

- Extend special courtesy toward those riding motor-cycles or bicycles. They are more exposed than persons in cars and more vulnerable in accidents.

Remember that the other person is likely not that different than your own mother, father, spouse, child, grandparent, or grandchild. Respond as you would want people to respond to those you love.

5. When someone else extends courtesy to you, respond with a wave and a smile if possible. If someone makes it easy for you to merge or grants you the right of way, reward them with a wave and a smile. Let that person know you appreciate the courtesy. Positive responses reinforce hospitality on the road and make the day more pleasant for everyone.

At the Airport

1. Allow plenty of time for the frustrations that are likely to be part of your airport experience. If local officials suggest arriving at the airport two hours before your flight, plan to be there two hours and fifteen minutes in advance. If you are not in danger of missing your flight, the delays caused by increased security and staff inefficiency will not be so hard to tolerate. If you are traveling alone, bring along a paperback book that you can read while standing in line or sitting in the gate area. That will help the time go by more easily and let you have the satisfaction of accomplishing something while you wait.

2. Make a firm decision that you are going to practice hospitality even if you are treated rudely by airport staff or other passengers. When we respond to the rudeness of others with rudeness of our own, situations escalate and become more unpleasant for everyone. When we remain calm and courteous, people are more likely to respond that way to us. Say a prayer for God's help in viewing security personnel as human beings like yourself who have difficult, stressful jobs.

3. Be alert for opportunities to show kindness to other travelers. Help elderly people with their luggage. Share your concern with people who have been upset because of rude treatment during the security screening process. Speak a kind word to an airline employee who appears to be having a bad day or who has just dealt with a difficult passenger. Be part of creating a warmer atmosphere rather than part of the problem.

4. Speak up when you experience treatment by airport personnel which is needlessly rude–but do it by letter rather than at the airport. If you express your frustration directly to security personnel, they are likely to react defensively and make the situation even more unpleasant. Part of the reason their behavior is so frustrating is that many of them haven't been well trained in how to interact with the public, and they are unlikely to respond positively to direct confrontation when they are in a position of authority. Note the name of the person if displayed on a tag or badge, the exact location, and the exact time of the incident. Write to airport or airline authorities describing what happened and suggesting an alternative approach. Send a copy of your letter to the mayor and a congressional representative. Your letter alone may not cause any change in behavior, but the impact of letters from large numbers of people can make a difference. If alternative airports are available to you without great inconvenience, then indicate that you will make a change in your future traveling plans if behaviors are not changed.

5. Share your appreciation when airport and airline personnel show courtesy and hospitality. Thank people for their courtesy. Tell them that you appreciate their doing a good job. Wish them a pleasant day. Smile at them. And write to airport or airline authorities to share your observations, mentioning employees by name.

It is probably wisest not to share words of appreciation in the middle of the screening process, because your motives may be misinterpreted by those doing the screening. They may believe you are being kind because you are trying to get away with something and subject you to greater scrutiny. That is a very sad consequence of the time in which we are living. Save your positive words until the process is over.

In the Neighborhood

1. If you don't know your closest neighbors, change that! Look for opportunities to introduce yourself to those who live around you. Don't be a pest and don't pry into their lives, but do seek opportunities to extend friendship. If you live in a large apartment complex in a major city, try smiling at people and saying "Good morning!" They may think you are strange at first, but most people in time will begin to respond in the same way.

2. Be alert for opportunities to show kindness to those who live near you. If someone's car won't start and you have jumper cables, help out! If someone's garbage can has fallen into the street, pick it up. If you live in an area where many leaves fall or snow accumulates, try raking the yard or shoveling the walk of a neighbor on an occasional basis. If your neighbor is elderly or has physical limitations, consider shoveling it all the time. If you learn that a neighbor has suffered a death in the family or has a loved one in the hospital, share your concern. Consider taking a baked dish to that neighbor's house as an expression of your sympathy. Bake cookies and take them to your neighbors at Christmas. Have a small open house with refreshments for your neighbors.

3. Pray for opportunities to become better acquainted with those who live near you. If you sincerely pray to God for help in knowing those who live near you, those opportunities are likely to come. God honors such prayers, and the act of praying will probably increase your sensitivity to those opportunities.

4. Remember that you don't have to become "best friends" with all your neighbors in order to benefit from knowing them. In the time in which we live, it certainly is true that our closest friendships are often with people from work, from community organizations, or from church. It may well be that you aren't going to form deep friendships with those whose primary tie to you is geographical proximity. But it is not socially or spiritually healthy to be completely disconnected from those who live nearby and whom you will see on at least an occasional basis. When you know your neighbors:

- You contribute to an overall environment of hospitality and good will which benefits everyone.

- Your neighbors are more likely to notice if there is a fire or a break-in at your home and to seek help. People who know each other pay more attention.

- Neighbors who know you will take a greater interest in the safety of your children.

- If you need help with car trouble, a plumbing emergency, or another household difficulty, there may well be a neighbor who can help you.

- You may have opportunities to be of help to your neighbors, and you will find your own life blessed as a result.

- You will find opportunities to be Christ's presence to those around you, and you will experience that presence from others.

The Workplace

1. Get to know the people with whom you interact through your work. This counsel may seem obvious, but millions of people in North America fail to do it! Increasing numbers of us work in large companies or organizations and interact with a significant number of people. Those of us who are self-employed have contact with clients, vendors, and subcontractors. It's easy to become accustomed to not remembering the names of those with whom we do business and to not knowing anything about people that isn't directly relevant to the business at hand.

Certainly many of us work in high pressure settings where time is at a premium. Lengthy visits with others can be inappropriate and irritating under such circumstances. That doesn't mean, however, that we shouldn't try to learn the names of those with whom we interact or endeavor, when appropriate, to learn more about them. Take advantage of opportunities which present themselves:

- If you've been encountering the same person in the same department or area for weeks or months or years and don't know that person's name, introduce yourself, say you're sorry you don't know that person's name, and share appreciation for the response. Perhaps you've been talking to the same person at the counter at a printer's office without knowing that person's name. Make an introduction. The other person will welcome it.

- If someone has an interesting poster or picture hanging in his or her workspace, share your appreciation.

- If people have pictures of their children, other family members, friends, or pets, ask about them.

- Although such things may seem trite, it is not inappropriate to ask if someone had a good weekend or had a good vacation or. . . .

2. When a coworker proves difficult or uncooperative, consider the possibility that the problem may not be related to you at all. When a coworker seems more difficult or resentful than usual, it's easy for us to jump to the conclusion that we must have done something wrong or at least something that is irritating to the other person. That's not always the case. Caring about others means being straight forward when necessary. You may want to say: "You seem upset about this project. Have I done something to make your work difficult?" OR "You seem more distressed than usual today. Is there anything I can help with?"

3. When you know that a coworker is going through a difficult time, gently express your concern. If a coworker has a family member who is ill or who has recently died, take a moment to stop by that person's workspace or make a phone call to express your concern. You don't have to initiate a lengthy conversation to make a difference. Simply say: "I was very sorry to learn that your father died. You'll be in my thoughts and prayers." Or "I just learned that your husband has been in the hospital. I want you to know that I am concerned and will be thinking about you." Be open to further conversation if the other person wants to talk.

Perhaps you have a coworker who failed to receive an anticipated promotion or who actually received a demotion. You may or may not know all the circumstances surrounding the decision. Usually, however, one can say something like: "I'm sorry that you didn't get the promotion. That must be very disappointing." OR "I'm sorry that you didn't get the promotion. I really enjoy working with you and value your contributions to the company." [Of course these may not be the best responses if you are the one who denied the promotion!]

4. When a coworker receives a promotion, an honor, or other special recognition, share your congratulations. We don't always think about sharing good wishes with others when good things happen to them. Many of us suffer from a little jealousy when something good happens to another person. But regardless of the circumstances, it's a good idea to congratulate others for the recognition they receive. Sharing our good wishes can help deepen relationships and can also help communication when things aren't so good.

Elisabeth Kübler-Ross tells the story of being named a "favorite professor" at the University of Chicago Medical School and being surprised when other faculty said nothing to her about the award. Then:

> *Toward the end of that day a gorgeous flower arrange-*
> *ment arrived at my office from one of my colleagues,*
> *a child psychiatrist. The card read, "Jealous as hell,*
> *congratulations anyway." From that moment on I*
> *knew I could trust that man. I loved him for being so*
> *real.* [In *Life Lessons* by Elisabeth Kübler-Ross and
> David Kessler, Simon and Schuster, 2000, p. 37]

We need to move beyond our feelings of competitiveness and jealousy to encounter others as real people, as potential blessings for our lives.

5. When you need to talk with a coworker about a problem, do so in the most positive and least judgmental way possible. That's true whether the person is your supervisor, an employee at the same level as yourself, a person you supervise, or a person in another department or with another firm. Be straightforward in identifying problems, but try to approach the issue as you would want another person to do with you. Remember that we all make mistakes, and none of us want to lose the respect of others because we've done something wrong. People find it easiest to correct mistakes and to change their approach to problems when difficult situations are presented to them in as positive a manner as possible.

6. Don't contribute to fear in the workplace. Some organizations seem to run on fear. The board fears the stockholders; the president fears the board, the vice presidents fear the president, and on down the line the fear continues to run. Fearful atmospheres don't tend to produce high creativity or longevity of employment. You may not be able to change the entire culture of your organization, but you can make a difference in your relationships with those with whom you most closely work. Avoid threatening people and putting people down. Treat others with respect, and encourage them to do the same in their interactions. Model a positive, caring, straightforward style. Refuse to be driven by fear.

7. Don't be a part of gossip or discrimination in the workplace (or anywhere else for that matter). It's not unusual in many work settings to hear statements like:

- "Did you hear how badly Ed got chewed out by the president? He won't be around here much longer."

- "I saw Mary looking pretty down in the mouth yesterday. Do you suppose she lost the Schmidt account? We'll all be in trouble if she did."

- "Did you know that Jim was in the hospital again last week? The way he looks, I just wonder if he has AIDS."

- "I know we've got all those equal employment opportunity laws to obey, but I don't think Pete fits in well here. There's just too much cultural difference."

- "Did you hear about Betty filing a sexual harassment complaint against her boss? I think she's been leading him on, trying to get a raise or a promotion, and she probably got just what she deserved."

No good purpose is served by those kinds of statements. Such opinions are often based on insufficient information and the human tendency to traffic in gossip. People can be deeply hurt by that kind of talk, because the more a statement is repeated, the more it is taken to be true. Even if statements like those just shared are true, spreading the information generally does nothing but hurt the persons who are involved.

A person who wants to practice true hospitality, who wants to recognize the presence of Christ in others, avoids saying things which may not be true, which can be hurtful, and which are not beneficial to the organization or the people involved.

8. Share compliments and positive messages when you have opportunity. You can make someone's day with just a few positive words, and you can contribute to an improved atmosphere in your organization. Try saying things like these:

- "Thanks for getting this job done for me so fast. I really feel under pressure on this project, and you've just made my life a lot easier."

- "By the way, I'm going to drop a note to the president and tell him what a great job you did on the presentation yesterday."

- "This report is excellent. Thanks so much for your work on it. I'm going to share it with several people."

- "I just learned that José and Margarita got the Meyers account for us. Their supervisor told me that they worked every evening and every weekend for a month to do it. That's going to make a big difference for our company. I'm going to thank them personally the next time I see them. You might want to say something to them too."

Dealing with Telephone Solicitations

1. Do your best to get OFF telephone solicitation lists (unless you actually like receiving these calls). Use services that put out lists of people who do not wish to be called. Take advantage of the "no call" lists which are available through some state governments. When you receive an unwanted solicitation call, tell the person who phones politely but firmly, "I make it a policy not to respond to telephone solicitations of any kind. It would be better for your company and better for me if you removed my name from your list."

Remember that when you order something in response to a telephone solicitation, you are practically guaranteeing that the same company will call you again and probably that your name and phone number will be sold to other companies as "an active telephone purchaser." If you really don't want to be bothered by telephone solicitations, then truly make it a policy not to order.

2. Remember that God does love the people who make telephone solicitations. Many of them would like to be earning their living in another way. Our being rude or irritable with them doesn't keep them from calling; it simply makes the whole experience worse for them and for us. Stay polite, but be firm in declining and in asking to be removed from their solicitation lists. When you hang up after an unwanted phone solicitation, say a prayer for the person with whom you have spoken, even if that person was irritating. The more irritating the person was and the more annoyed you became, the more important the prayer!

3. Make a distinction between solicitation calls for sales from companies and solicitation calls for donations from organizations with which you are connected. The student calling from the college or university from which you graduated or the neighbor calling on behalf of United Way should not get the same response as the person wanting to put aluminum siding on your brick house. While declining all sales solicitation calls is a wise move, you may want to remain open to some charitable calls. Remember, however, that some charitable organizations will sell your name to others. If you don't want your name shared, you may wish to say: "I'm happy to give you a donation, but I want to make it clear that I do not want my name given to any other organization."

E-mail and the Internet

1. Never say anything in an e-mail that you would not say in a face-to-face conversation or over the telephone. Rude is rude. Discourteous is discourteous. Insensitive is insensitive–in e-mail or any other medium. Reflecting anger in an e-mail message is commonly known as "flaming" in Internet circles, and people always resent it. Like an angry printed letter, an angry electronic letter can continue to hang around for months and years and may be used against you at a future time. While delaying a response in order to cool off may clutter your electronic mailbox or computer file folders, it will help you avoid the series of electronic correspondence or personal conversations required to make peace later. Even if you don't know someone, remember that strangers over the Internet are the children of God just like strangers in your neighborhood or anywhere else. You want your interactions with others to be a blessing to their lives, not a curse.

2. Recognize that while they should not, people will sometimes say things in e-mail that they won't in printed mail. The process of producing printed mail takes longer and gives more time for thought. When someone sends you a flaming piece of e-mail, don't take offense too quickly and don't escalate the conflict by responding in the same way. That person may self-correct if given time.

3. If you have a computer or are considering one, remember that e-mail can be a powerful medium for staying in contact with people about whom you care. It's great to look in your electronic mail box and see that your parent, child, spouse, grandparent, brother, sister, or friend has sent you e-mail. Many parents find it a very economical and convenient way to stay in touch with sons and daughters who are in college. Friends, whether in the same city or across the country or around the world, often choose e-mail for the convenience and economy of the medium.

E-mail blends some of the best characteristics of a letter delivered through the mail and a phone call without some of the problems. A letter received through the mail lets the recipient read it at a convenient time, and e-mail does the same. You don't have to respond the second it comes as you do with a phone call. On the other hand, e-mail is much faster than a letter sent through the mail. When the computers and servers that transmit the e-mail are all working smoothly, e-mail communication can jump across the country or around the world at about the same speed as a phone call. The cost of sending e-mail is normally built into whatever monthly fee you pay for connection to the Internet. That makes e-mail much more timely than a letter through the mail service and much less expensive than a phone call (unless you start to count the cost of the computer, the modem, and the software!).

4. While you certainly want to urge your children to be cautious about building relationships on the Internet, be aware that common interests discovered through this medium can be very rewarding for adults. One of the neatest things about the Internet is that there are so many people who are willing to help others and who are very generous with their time and knowledge. Questions posted to Internet bulletin boards or shared with electronic mail groups can bring you a tremendous amount of helpful information. While you may spend some time personally responding to inquiries in an electronic mail group to which you belong, you need to balance that expenditure of time with the benefit of ideas others share with you through that electronic group or in response to your bulletin board inquiries. You have many opportunities to share hospitality through this electronic medium, and you can be the positive recipient of the hospitality of others.

Business and Community Contacts

1. Treat waiters, waitresses, cashiers, tellers, and others courteously, recognizing that they embody the presence of our Lord. It's easy not to think much about our interactions with the people who serve us in stores, banks, restaurants, and other commercial settings. The personnel in these positions often change rapidly, and it is not realistic to think that we will build significant relationships with many of these persons. We'll only see some of them a single time.

We don't need to have a significant discussion each time we interact with a person while transacting a small amount of business; but we can use those opportunities to display friendliness, warmth, and good humor. Doing so can make a difference. Here's an example of a friend named Ruth's interactions as she spent a Friday afternoon running errands:

- When she got a quick lunch at McDonald's, she noticed that the clerk had obviously spent a long time painting elaborate designs on her fingernails. Ruth's first thought was "this person has nothing better to do with her time than paint her nails. What a waste." Then Ruth considered the possibility that the clerk had few things that made her feel good about herself. Ruth said to her, "The design on your nails is very intriguing. Did it take a lot of work to do that?" The clerk beamed with appreciation and told Ruth that she and her sister spent one evening a week doing each other's nails. Ruth brought pleasure to the woman and also learned that the elaborately decorated nails were linked to a family activity.

- There was a long line for the drive-through at the bank. As she sat in the line, Ruth remembered that it was the first day of the month, when many people receive their payroll or pension payments. She reflected to herself that a lot of those people needed direct deposit and an ATM card. Then she recognized that she was wanting to transfer money among some accounts and get bills of a particular denomination for graduation gifts. Others in the line could have similar needs. When Ruth's turn came, the teller greeted her over the intercom system. Ruth said back to her, "It looks like you're having a very busy day. I hope it's a good one for you." The teller responded, with added warmth in her voice, "The first of the month is always a challenge. I hope you didn't have to wait in line long." And even though Ruth had waited in line what seemed like a long time, both she and the teller felt better because of the warm exchange.

- At the Post Office, Ruth wanted to get self-stick stamps with a pink rose design. The clerk who waited on her said, "I don't have those. You can have flags or fruit, no roses." There were several other postal clerks, and Ruth wondered if one of them might have roses. She was tempted to be demanding, but then decided to use a different approach. With a smile on her face and warmth in her voice, Ruth said, "I know you have to feel swamped with all the people coming in here, but my husband and I really like using the rose design on our envelopes. Is there any possibility that another clerk might have some and that you could get them from that person?" The clerk smiled back, asked another clerk for the stamps, and then sold them to Ruth. Ruth thanked both the clerks, who wished her a good day.

- At a superstore offering a wide variety of products, Ruth had difficulty finding the kind of light bulbs she needed and asked a clerk for help. The clerk immediately stopped stocking shelves and took Ruth to another section of light bulbs. Ruth thanked the clerk for her help and asked her how she liked working in the store. The clerk thanked Ruth for her interest and told her that it was a good place to work for a second income but that the pay wasn't enough to support a family. They shared a few additional words, and Ruth said a silent prayer for the clerk and her family as she went on with her shopping.

- Ruth stopped by the dry cleaner on her way home. She had been going to the same place for five years and was on a first name basis with the two clerks who worked there. Sylvia, the clerk who waited on Ruth this time, seemed visibly distressed. Ruth said to her, "You seem upset today, Sylvia. Is anything wrong?" And Sylvia responded by sharing a few of the problems she was having with her 14-year-old son who had a court appearance to make the following Monday. The store started to fill with customers so further conversation was going to be awkward, but Ruth invited Sylvia to call her at home that evening if she wanted to talk more. Sylvia did call her that night, initially just to thank Ruth for her concern, but she then proceeded to share more of her situation. Since Sylvia did not have a church home, Ruth suggested that she consider calling the youth pastor at Ruth's church because of that pastor's experience working with troubled young people.

Ruth improved the quality of her own day and the quality of the day for several others by the way in which she interacted as she conducted her business. The most significant discussion, of course, was with Sylvia. That discussion would not have been likely if Ruth had not built a good relationship over the years.

2. Develop a healthy interest in others, learn to ask questions, and listen. Many of Ruth's positive interactions came because she was genuinely interested in the people with whom she did business. She asked one person about her nails; she asked another person what it was like to work in the store; and she asked Sylvia if anything was wrong. She received a response each time, and she listened with genuine interest. People are hungry for positive connection with others. When we develop an interest in the people around us and ask the right questions, we'll learn a great deal and find our lives enriched as a result.

3. Say prayers for the persons with whom you interact, even when you do not know their names. Ruth said a silent prayer for the clerk in the superstore, and she also prayed for Sylvia. Ruth has also prayed more than once for patience before going into her Post Office branch because of the negative attitudes she has found there. At the end of each day, Ruth has the habit of praying for each person she has encountered and seeking God's help and direction for the new day.

4. Learn to look for and expect the best in others rather than the worst. When we experience service which is repeatedly indifferent or poor, our sense of expectation gets pulled down. It's easy to reach a point at which we no longer expect to be treated well by others and as a result do not treat them well. We can't change the attitudes which other people have, but we can change our own. That can be the starting point in creating a more civil, hospitable society.

Simple resolutions to be "friendlier" won't result in deep change in our habits or in the attitudes of others. What's needed is a sincere desire to recognize the presence of Christ in the lives of the people with whom we do business and to respond to them appropriately.

From a business perspective, there's nothing "weak" about this approach. When we expect the best from others, we truly want to find it. While being critical of people doesn't help them, clearly asking for what we want does. There's nothing inhospitable about saying things like:

- "I'm sorry, but this fish isn't well enough done for me. I would appreciate your having this cooked a little more thoroughly."

- "I know that you want to do the right thing. I thought this shirt would be the right size for my brother, but I was wrong. I need for you to accept it as a return."

- "I still have the same problem with my car's heating system that I did when I brought it to you for service last week. This problem is apparently a difficult one to fix. As you're working to repair it, I'd appreciate your keeping in mind that I've already paid a substantial amount. I'm hoping not to have another bill today unless there are other parts that are needed."

- "I know the dentist's practice is very busy, and it must be difficult to get everyone scheduled. I am worried about my son's tooth. He doesn't often complain but seems in a lot of pain this time. I don't see how he can wait two weeks for an appointment. Would it be possible for us to come late in the day or early in the morning when regular appointments aren't scheduled? My son and I would really appreciate your asking the dentist about that possibility."

In each instance just shared, the speaker is firm about the need for service but is also respectful of the other person and does not immediately assume bad intentions on the part of the other person.

Practice Hospitality Wherever Possible

Fred is always positively impressed when he visits the office of his financial planner. The greeting is consistently warm, and the receptionist immediately asks if Fred would like coffee. Coffee, tea, cream, sugar, cups, and spoons are always available, making it clear that guests are expected at this place of business. Certainly one can take the view that "it's good for business to have refreshments," and that's no doubt true. Fred would still be going to the financial planner, however, even if no coffee were served. The fact that it is served increases the sense of welcome and makes the business transaction more pleasant.

Most of us should think about the opportunities we have to deepen our hospitality to those around us: to clients, coworkers, neighbors, friends, and family. Where can we add hospitality without slowing down a busy day? Where should we make a conscious effort to slow the pace of the day for a few minutes? Could you increase the level of hospitality in your life by:

- Having a dish of candy on your desk to share with coworkers and clients?

- Offering a cup of hot chocolate to the mail delivery person on a cold winter day?

- Asking the neighbor who is collecting signatures on a petition for a neighborhood improvement to share with you in a soft drink or a cup of coffee?

- Inviting a person you would like to know better to have breakfast or lunch with you?

- Inviting a person who seems to spend too much time alone to share a meal in your home?

Sharing the Faith

Both of us have written and taught about ways to share the faith with others and to invite others to participate in the life of the church. That's not our primary focus in this book, though the concluding chapter does deal with hospitality within the faith community. The relationships we build through the practice of hospitality can provide a basis for us to visit with others about the faith, about what God means in our lives. Sometimes we fail to recognize the opportunities for such discussions when they come.

Unhealthy practices of evangelism in our society may have blocked our own willingness to witness to what is most important in our lives. Ruth would not have felt comfortable handing an evangelism tract to the clerk at McDonald's or at the Post Office. On the other hand, she was certainly willing to visit about faith issues with Sylvia on the telephone because that was directly relevant to Sylvia's concerns.

When we focus on recognizing the presence of Christ in others, then we will have opportunities to talk about the role that faith plays in our lives. We do not have to be manipulative in order for those openings to come; God will bring them to us if we are open to receiving them.

In a time of fear and suspicion toward those who hold different faiths, it is important for our words and actions to communicate respect for those who express their belief in different ways than we do. Dialogue with those of the Islamic faith can bring blessings to our own lives.

To Avoid Being a Crime Victim

- Keep a list of your credit card numbers and the phone numbers to report their theft readily accessible.

- Never let someone have both your social security number and your credit card number. That makes it very easy for someone to get additional information about you and to steal your identity. If a clerk in a hotel or store asks to see a photo-ID to go with your credit card, show them your license, but cover up the social security number when you do so.

- If you put your purse or packages in the trunk of your car, move the car before you continue shopping. Thieves watch for people putting items in their trunks and then going back into a shopping center.

- Don't carry unnecessary cash. With bank machines available all over North America and Europe, you don't need large amounts of cash when traveling.

- Don't share your credit card number with someone over the phone unless YOU initiated the phone call.

- Check your credit card statements for unauthorized charges.

- Lights and a dog continue to be good ways to discourage residential burglaries. Illuminated entries and lights around the house make it harder to force entry and make the home appear occupied. Use lights on timers when you are gone. And–burglars don't like dogs.

Chapter Eight:
Hospitality and the Hurting

> **Concept:** We need to discover what hospitality can mean for the poor, for race relations, for those struggling with drug and alcohol problems, for criminals and crime victims, and for others in our society who are hurting.

In *Angela's Ashes*, Frank McCourt describes the hospitality frequently shown by his mother and by others who were horribly poor. When food was difficult to find and extremely expensive, a woman in a store gave Frank's mother an onion for their sick child. A butcher sold Frank's family a pig's head for Christmas and then gave them some sausage for their Christmas breakfast.

Even though their own financial situation was so bleak that the gifts of an onion and of sausage were significant, Frank's mother always found a way to respond to others in need:

> You never know when you might come home and find
> Mam sitting by the fire chatting with a woman and a child,
> strangers. Always a woman and child. Mam finds them
> wandering the streets and if they ask, Could you spare
> a few pennies, miss? her heart breaks. She never has
> money so she invites them home for tea and a bit of friend
> bread and if it's a bad night she'll let them sleep by the
> fire on a pile of rags in the corner. The bread she
> gives them always means less for us and if we complain
> she says there are always people worse off and we can
> surely spare a little from what we have. [p. 273]

When Frank McCourt was older and began delivering telegrams, he discovered that those to whom he made the deliveries often begged for assistance. His supervisors told him firmly that he must never do anything but deliver the telegram. Yet he found himself bringing telegram money orders to people who were starving and who were physically unable to do anything with the money order. They would beg Frank to get the money order cashed for them and to buy them some groceries. If he got on his bicycle and left, he would be leaving them with a money order that was useless. Thus he found himself disobeying his employers in order to help people who were starving.

While we may not be exposed to physical needs that seem as extreme as those described eloquently by McCourt, we live in a world filled with hurting people. If we believe that Christ's presence is in others, then we have a responsibility to reach out to those persons. Although none of us individually can solve the pressing social problems of our world, each of us can make a contribution. Frank's mother, even in her times of deepest poverty, found a way to respond to persons in need; and Frank himself learned that rules were not as important as compassion.

Partly because of the fear of our time, many of us live in isolation from people with certain kinds of needs. Most of us live in neighborhoods populated by people of about our same income level and often our same ethnic background. Some of us have elaborate security systems to keep others away. If we are middle class, upper middle class, or wealthy, we may have relatively little exposure to persons who live in deep poverty or who have different ethnic backgrounds. Many of us do not have a close relationship with a person who has a serious disability.

As this book is about to go to press, the latest revisions put the death toll from the September 11, 2001 terrorist attacks at around 4,000 people. Those losses are tragic and have truly affected everyone in North America. The images of the planes crashing into the towers of the World Trade Center are burned into the minds of all of us. There are other daily tragedies, however, which do not receive comparable publicity or impact our lives in the same way. The Food and Agricultural Organization of the United Nations estimates that 9,000,000 people a year die from hunger–that's 24,000 a day. Most of those deaths do not come from actual starvation but from the severe malnutrition and poor resistance to disease that accompany hunger.

There are also shocking statistics for deaths from drunk driving, abortions, firearm accidents, homicides, suicides, and other tragedies. AIDS, cancer, heart disease, and other illnesses claim lives every hour. The death rate, of course, stands at 100%. Life ends for all of us eventually, but we are rightly distressed when death comes earlier or more painfully than expected.

And we know that suffering is not limited to death and grief. The lives of people are changed each day because of child abuse, rape, and other acts of violence. Addictions to alcohol and other drugs ruin the lives of people of all ages, and eating disorders affect millions in North America.

The very magnitude of the statistics is part of the problem. Most of us have difficulty grasping the full horror of 4,000 people dying in the events of September 11, 2001. Numbers like 24,000 deaths from hunger each day of the year are beyond our comprehension.

Overwhelmed by information from the media and from charitable organizations about the problems of our time, we unconsciously block out much of the information we receive. None of us alone can have significant impact on even one of these problems. The outpouring of generosity toward the victims of the terrorist attacks and their families, however, stands as a strong reminder that we have the power to do more than we realize.

The World Health Organization has estimated that thirteen billion dollars a year would end hunger for the poorest people on earth. That is a large sum of money, but the United States quickly appropriated twenty billion to deal with the destruction in New York City, knowing that more would be needed. And to put this in further perspective, people in North America and Europe spend eighteen billion dollars a year on pet food.

Called to Reach Out

No matter where we live, there are of course persons with significant needs who live close to us. Even the most affluent neighborhoods have young people who are alienated from their families, single parents, persons struggling with drug and alcohol problems, and elderly persons who spend too much time alone. We need to develop a greater sensitivity to the needs of the persons with whom we are in contact on a regular basis. Much of this book, especially the preceding chapter, has talked about cultivating a greater openness to others and a greater willingness to respond to the needs of those around us.

153

At the same time, we need to recognize that there are persons with significant needs with whom we may not come in much contact. Most of us are not going to deliver telegrams to a person who lives in poverty and thus are not going to have the opportunity to respond which Frank McCourt did.

At a conference of Christian leaders, Steve Clapp asked 300 persons how many of them had a person of a different race as one of their four or five closest friends. Only 22 hands went up. Should we be surprised that there are so many tensions between blacks and whites or among other races when our friendship circles are not more diverse? Only 20 of those present had a person of a non-Christian religion as one of their closest friends. Should we be surprised at the lack of understanding between Muslims and Christians?

Most of us need to stretch our comfort zones if we are going to make a difference on some of the pressing social problems and justice issues of our time. Those problems should not be viewed as belonging exclusively to government agencies or social service organizations. If all persons are our brothers and sisters in Christ, then we need to be reaching out to those who are in need, even when they do not live in our neighborhoods. In *Reaching Out*, Henri Nouwen reminds us that:

> *From the point of view of a Christian spirituality,*
> *it is important to stress that every human being is*
> *called upon to be a healer* [p. 65].

When we let our fears and the demands of our lives keep us from being involved with persons who are different from ourselves, we contribute to a society which is far from hospitable for vast numbers of persons. We also fail to receive the blessings God waits to give us when we begin to seek interaction with those who are different from ourselves.

Hospitality and Justice Systems

Before the terrorist attacks, no single issue in North America embodied our corporate fears so much as the problem of crime and the equally large problem of the criminal justice systems which are to combat crime. No one wants to be a victim of crime! A partial list of strategies for protection are given on the page opposite the beginning of this chapter. Most of us can readily add other cautions to that list.

As discussed earlier in this book, politicians and the media have had much to gain by making us acutely aware of the dangers posed to us by crime. Violent crime in the United States certainly is a major problem–far more so than, for example, in Canada. We all want to feel safe, and it's easy for us to be strongly influenced by political rhetoric and thirty-second sound bites. The facts about crime and about criminal justice systems are more complicated. Consider some information that isn't included in most political rhetoric:

Juvenile Crime

In the 1990s almost every state in the U.S. passed laws to transfer more young people to adult courts. A study funded by the Walter S. Johnson Foundation in partnership with a large coalition including the National Crime Prevention Council found that those strategies do not work. For example:

- Youth offenders transferred to adult court re-offend more often and with more serious offenses than those who stay in the juvenile system.

- Youth in adult institutions are eight times more likely to commit suicide, five times more likely to be sexually assaulted, and fifty percent more likely to be attacked with a weapon than youth in juvenile institutions.

- The majority of youth transferred to adult courts spend months waiting on trial, at a cost to taxpayers of around $200 a day.

- But youth in juvenile institutions also have problems and have relatively high rates of being arrested again. An approach called Functional Family Therapy which works with youth and their families in their homes has reduced repeated offenses by 25% to 80%. It costs much less than incarceration in an adult or a juvenile facility.

You can find out more about juvenile justice issues in an excellent report titled *Less Hype, More Help* which is available online at www.aypf.org or through the American Youth Policy Forum at the address given in the *Resources* section of this book.

Problems in Jails and Prisons

Dr. Chris Schriner, a Unitarian pastor in California, reminded his congregation in a sermon of some of the consequences of our lack of concern about what happens to those convicted of crimes:

> *Our society has never provided adequate oversight of jails and prisons. Voters don't clamor for independent watchdogs who protect prisoner's rights. In fact some people hope that prisoners will have unpleasant experiences so they won't want to go back to jail. But few of us know just how badly prisoners are treated, and we may not have thought about how repeated abuse leads to anger and depression, making convicts less likely to be positive members of society when they are released.*

The Los Angeles Times, in the summer of 1998, had a series of articles on the use of force by prison guards: "The guards always gave the same paradoxical reason for resorting to deadly force. They were trying to stop fights from turning deadly. In all but a few cases [in which guards had shot prisoners to death] internal reports show, the inmates did not carry weapons or cause so much as a swollen lip while brawling."

The same series talks about violence against inmates arriving at one California prison. When a new bus pulled in, "dozens of guards snapped into drill position and performed a half-hour of football-like warmups and cheers. Wearing black gloves and tape over their name tags, the officers grabbed shackled inmates one-by-one and ran them through a gauntlet of fists, batons, and combat boots. One inmate was thrown through a window, another rammed into a wall." The same article talks about a prison at Corcoran where "problem inmates were purposely locked into a cell and subjected to repeated rapes by an inmate enforcer." That leads one to ask who the real criminals are: Those who have been sentenced? Or those who run the prisons where they are sent?

Most of us would prefer not to know too much about the problems within the criminal justice system. We don't want to consider the possibility that those in prison may be abused, and we certainly don't want to consider the possibility that the systems which exist to protect us sometimes convict those who are innocent.

Severe Sentences

California, like some other states, passed a "three strikes" law (three felonies and you go to jail for at least twenty years before parole eligibility). The first person sentenced under that law in Orange County was Joyce Demyers. She was a drug addict who had been arrested for robbery and burglary. Her third strike came in a sting in which she helped carry out a cocaine purchase between a drug dealer and a plainclothes policeman. Her cut of the deal was $5.00. Her sentence was 25 years to life. If she serves the minimum amount of the sentence and stays physically healthy, she will cost the state of California at least $420,000. Dr. Schriner suggested that for that sum of money, she could have a personal supervisor who spent time with her each day. That would seem absurd, but spending half a million dollars to keep her locked up also seems absurd.

While California has been singled out in some of these examples, similar problems exist all over the United States. We have been convinced that severe sentences would result in our streets and our neighborhoods being safer, and we have not thought about the consequences of those sentences.

Our Brothers and Sisters

In fact we have not thought about the persons who commit crimes as being our brothers and sisters in Christ. Most of us have been comfortable thinking of criminals as persons who are fundamentally different than the rest of us. With that in mind, we feel safest separating those persons from the rest of society. In *The Gulag Archipelago*, Alexander Solzhenitsyn, writing about his experiences while incarcerated by the former Soviet Union, reminds us:

> *Gradually it was disclosed to me that the line*
> *separating good and evil passes not through*
> *states, nor between classes, nor between parties*
> *either–but right through every human heart–*
> *through all human hearts.*

The prophet Jeremiah reminds us of the same reality: "The heart is deceitful above all things, and desperately wicked: who can know it?" [Jeremiah 17:9, KJV]. It is not possible to neatly separate the "good" people from the "bad" people, because the line between good and bad runs through each of our hearts. If we wanted to purge all evil from society, we would each have to tear out a pieces of ourselves.

What would it mean for us to truly recognize the presence of Christ in each person? What would that mean in terms of our relationships with the victims of crime, the police, and persons convicted of crimes? A full answer to the question is a topic for another book, but here are some thoughts from the perspective of hospitality:

1. Reaching out to young people, before they are in serious trouble with the law, is probably the best single strategy to make our society safer. Church youth programs; Boys and Girls Clubs; scouting; Big Brothers, Big Sisters; and other community organizations have the potential to make a difference. Almost all of these organizations are continually seeking volunteers. There are creative court programs in some parts of North America which need volunteers to take a special interest in young people just starting to get into trouble. Could God be calling you to show hospitality to a young person through one of these programs? Certainly financial support and prayers for these efforts are important, but direct involvement offers many blessings to young people and to adults who help.

2. We need to show a true spirit of hospitality toward those persons who are the victims of crime. People who have been robbed, assaulted, stalked, embezzled, raped, or otherwise injured through the conduct of other people often, understandably, find it difficult to trust others and difficult not to be filled with bitterness for what happened to them. Our willingness to listen, our efforts to understand, and our demonstrations of kindness and acceptance can make a difference for those who have been victims.

3. City and county law enforcement officers are on the front lines of crime prevention, and they need our affirmation and our encouragement. They are the visible presence in most of our communities which can help lower crime and can help all of us feel safer. Their jobs are difficult, and their work is often not appreciated. There are serious problems of racial profiling and abuse of power by law enforcement officers, but the abuse of authority by some should not be permitted to reflect badly on all. People who care about justice need to build relationships with persons in law enforcement. When people spend forty hours a week or longer working heavily with persons who do not obey the law, it's easy to become cynical. The active friendship of ordinary people lets law enforcement personnel know they are appreciated and helps them keep perspective.

4. We need to show hospitality to persons who have been convicted of crimes and to their families. If we keep in mind the reality that these persons are our brothers and sisters in Christ, then we can reach out with concern and compassion. When people we know or family members of people we know are charged with crimes, we can be a caring, supportive, nonjudgmental presence in their lives. People who are incarcerated need visitors, letters, and prayers. Their family members are likewise in need of friendship and help.

5. We should seek to be informed about criminal justice issues, to put less faith in the rhetoric of politicians, and to work for genuine reform. When justice systems fail to work and perpetuate problems rather than bring healing, those systems need to be changed. Again, a spirit of hospitality means recognizing the presence of Christ in victims of crime, in those charged with crimes, in law enforcement personnel, and (even) in politicians. Those of us who believe firmly in that presence have the ability to be advocates for changes which create a healthier society.

Too Many Issues

We've devoted a few pages of this book to the discussion of issues within the criminal justice system. Obviously a full book could be devoted to examining those problems from the perspective of hospitality. We chose to focus on criminal justice issues because the fear of crime is one of the dominant forces shaping much of our contemporary life and working against the practice of hospitality for many people.

No one person can become immersed in every issue which exists. To thoroughly discuss each of the major issues of our time would require a series of books. Looking at those issues and at the persons whose lives are affected by them from the perspective of hospitality does have the potential to transform our society. It's not important that each one of us attempts to tackle every social issue that exists. It is important that we learn how to look at issues from the perspective of hospitality, to recognize the presence of Christ in others. It's also important that we select one or two specific ways in which we can reach out and be a healing presence in society. In addition to the suggestions made in the discussion of criminal justice issues, consider these possibilities:

- Develop a relationship with one person or with one family in poverty. You may do it through a formal mentoring program of a church or a social service agency, or you may choose to do it on your own with a person or family you encounter.

- Become active in an organization which is working to change the root causes of poverty. Volunteer time, give financial support, and consider being on the board of directors. Bring a perspective of hospitality to the organization.

- Develop a friendship with a person or a family of another ethnic background. Again, it's possible to do this through formal programs in some communities, but it may be most meaningful if you develop such a relationship on your own.

- Cultivate a relationship with a person of the Islamic faith. Come to understand the differences and the similarities between that faith and your own. Use the information you gain to help others better understand the Islamic faith.

- Become active in an organization which is working to improve race relations. In most communities there is a particularly great need for efforts involving black–

white relationships. If no organizations are doing work in this area, consider the possibility of initiating some efforts yourself!

- Develop a friendship with a person who is disabled. Do not look at the relationship as one in which you are going to provide the "help" but rather as one in which each of you will receive blessings. If you are disabled yourself, seek opportunities to help those who are not disabled feel comfortable around you and begin to identify with you as a person who has a disability rather than being focused on the disability itself.

- Build a relationship with an elderly person who does not have family living nearby. This could be a person in your neighborhood or in your church. Include that person in your family life, and use the opportunity to learn from that person's life experiences.

- Volunteer to work at a women's shelter. Create friendships and help women who have been in abusive relationships as they seek to build their self-confidence and ability to trust others. This can be a wonderful opportunity to show hospitality to people for whom it can make a difference.

And the list could be continued. Remember, none of us can do everything. All of us can do something. As a life grounded in hospitality causes us to recognize the presence of Christ in others, we should be willing to reach out beyond our normal circle of acquaintances and friends. There are angels to be found and blessings to be received.

Congregations and Hospitality

- In a Christian Community study of churches across North America, 85% of the church members surveyed agreed with this statement: "In our congregation, people go out of their way to be friendly to strangers and new-comers." In growing churches, 98% agreed.

- In the same study, people were asked to indicate agree-ment with the more personal statement: "At church, I take the initiative to talk with those I do not know well." The level of agreement dropped to 68% on this item among all people who participated but only dropped to 92% in growing congregations. In rapidly declining churches, the level of agreement was often below 50%.

- When asked in that study how welcome a person with a drug or alcohol problem would be in the congregation, 90% of those in growing churches said such a person would be warmly welcomed. Only 38% of those in declining churches felt that way.

- 95% of those in growing churches felt that a single parent would find a warm welcome; the figure drops to 62% in churches which are in decline.

- While the size of the church, the programs of the church, the personality of the minister, and many other factors play a role in the interest of people in joining, no single factor is as important as the answer to this question: Is this a friendly church? Is this a church which understands and believes in hospitality?

- In another Christian Community study, only 8% of the participating churches had offered a class or seminar to help members better understand other faiths such as Judaism, Islam, Buddhism, and Hinduism.

Chapter Nine:
Hospitality and the
Faith Community

> **Concept:** Hospitality should be at the heart of the
> faith community and has the power to transform
> congregational life. Churches can help people deal
> with their fears and reach out to others.

Christian churches and other religious congregations
around the country showed strong responses to the events of
September 11, 2001:

- Special services of prayer and remembrance were held
  in congregations around North America and indeed all
  around the world.

- Christian ministers and other clergy attempted to
  address some of the difficult questions raised by those
  attacks. Why does evil exist? Why does God permit
  freedom great enough to let such horrid things happen?
  How well does God actually protect us?

- Attendance went up in most congregations as vast
  numbers of people sought the consolation of worship
  and reflected on questions of life and death.

- Both ecumenical and denominational emergency
  relief agencies sought financial assistance from
  congregations as they attempted to respond to the
  suffering in New York and Washington. The responses
  from congregations were generous.

- Some congregations had volunteers who stood watch
  at mosques to be sure that these Islamic houses of
  prayer were not vandalized and that those coming to
  worship were not harassed. Christian volunteers in
  some cities accompanied Muslim people who wear
  traditional dress so that they would feel safe going to

the store, to school, and to places of employment.
These acts of hospitality helped strengthen bonds
between Christian and Muslim people.

The fears which people hold, however, are not easily relieved;
and many of our deepest religious questions do not have simple
answers. As we move on from terrorist attacks and threats, the
fears and the questions continue to be with us.

This book has been addressed more to individuals than to
congregations. Only this final chapter looks primarily at a congregational perspective on hospitality. Beyond the practice of a
broad hospitality, there are some other strategies through which
congregations can help people living in a fearful time:

- People don't want to hear simple answers to complex
  problems–but they do need to hear affirmation of the
  basic truths of the faith: that Christ loves us and is
  with us in difficult times; that God is ultimately
  victorious over evil; and that God hears our prayers.
  Many people continue to live in fear, and these core
  beliefs speak to those fears. People need to be
  reminded that courage is not the absence of fear but
  doing the right thing in spite of fear.

- People need opportunities to discuss their fears and
  anxieties about terrorism. Encourage classes and
  groups to begin with a time for the sharing of joys
  and concerns. The need for this kind of sharing exists
  for children, youth, and adults. The sharing time
  shouldn't be introduced as a focus on terrorism or
  fear but rather as an open time in which people can
  raise whatever joys or concerns they have.

- Provide opportunities for people to learn about the
  Islamic faith and to have contact with Muslims. There
  are six to ten million Muslims in North America and
  perhaps a billion around the world. We need to understand their faith and to recognize how thoroughly
  the extremists have perverted that faith in using it as
  a justification for violence. Churches can be wonderful
  forums for such study and contact.

- Churches need to be concerned about the actions of others toward Muslim people in North America and around the world. We need to raise questions about military actions which harm civilians and about the circumstances under which people are detained for questioning. Being a true patriot means expecting the very best from other citizens and from political and military leaders.

- Offer classes on hospitality, which has the power to transform how we feel about God, other people, and ourselves. Resources like this book and *Widening the Welcome of Your Church* can help in that process.

- Let people in the community know about programs in the church on understanding the Islamic faith, on dealing with fear, and on practicing hospitality. Use positive publicity so that those outside the church know what the congregation offers.

- Offer classes which help people talk about their faith and learn how to more effectively share it with others. Talking about the faith can help in dealing with fear.

- Use e-mail to share weekly devotions with members and nonmembers. Speak to issues of faith, fear, and hospitality in those devotions. Encourage prayers for the nation, for those harmed by the events of September 11, 2001, for other victims of terrorism, and for the impoverished people of Afghanistan and the world.

- Offer children, youth, and adults opportunities to raise money to help others and to practice kindness. People focused on doing positive things are less likely to be overwhelmed by the negative.

The suggestions just offered and those which follow are addressed primarily to Christians and Christian congregations, because that is the faith with which we are most familiar. We do know that the basic elements of hospitality are present in all the major religions of the world, and we also recognize that all the religious traditions have teachings which can help people develop their spiritual lives and deal with the fears which threaten to immobilize them. While this book is addressed primarily to those of Christian orientation, we hope that some of the strategies will be helpful to those of other traditions.

For the remainder of this chapter, we invite you to reflect with us on some of the important elements of hospitality in congregational life. How can our churches truly welcome people and equip them to reach out to others?

The Search for Hospitality

Yusuf and Andrea are, to some, an unusual couple because Yusuf grew up in the Muslim faith and Andrea grew up as a Protestant Christian. Both of their families were initially less than enthusiastic about their marriage. They loved each other, but neither one wanted to convert. They are determined to maintain their respective faiths, to be supportive of each other, and to let any children they may have make their own faith choices after exposure to both traditions.

Yusuf began attending church with Andrea and found himself very much enjoying the discussions in the young adult class they attended together. While he had a different view of the nature of Jesus, Yusuf respected the Christian faith and felt that he learned a great deal from the class sessions. The members of the young adult class, who all became friends with Yusuf, had no difficulty accepting him and appreciated the perspective that he brought to their discussions.

The discomfort for Yusuf came when he interacted with older members of the congregation during the fellowship time and after worship services. He noticed the strange looks on the faces of those who learned that he was attending with Andrea but was in fact a Muslim. Following the events of September 11, 2001, Yusuf began to feel that people looked at him with suspicion. Andrea tried to tell him that he was too sensitive, but she was dismayed when one person asked him in the fellowship time, "Explain to me, please, how it is that your faith teaches that it's all right to take the lives of innocent people."

Yusuf responded by saying that the terrorists horribly misinterpreted the teachings of Islam, which absolutely did not support such acts of violence. He said that Muslim people around the world were horribly upset about what had happened and that, as a United States citizen, he was outraged by the terrorist attacks. The person who had challenged him responded by saying, "Well, you ought to consider leaving your religion so no one would think you agreed with Osama bin Laden."

Yusuf had felt like suggesting that his interrogator might want to leave the Christian faith in order to make it clear that he did not agree with those who bombed abortion clinics. Yusuf, however, simply walked away, feeling there was no way to have a satisfactory conclusion to the conversation. He and Andrea did not return to the church.

Kristen, a friend and colleague of both Fred and Steve, moved with her husband to a new community immediately after they married. Kristen's roots were in the Quaker and the Church of the Brethren traditions; her husband Chad had grown up in a Disciples of Christ congregation. The two of them began searching for a church home in their new community.

A large number of resources, including some Steve and Fred have written, emphasize the importance of churches making a prompt response to visitors and point out that a letter from the pastor, while a nice gesture, isn't a sufficient response. One of the suggestions frequently made is that a volunteer from the church take a gift of baked goods such as cookies or a loaf of bread to the people who visited. It's a simple thing to do and an excellent way to convey interest in the visitors.

Kristen and Chad, however, were not receiving any cookies! Several months and many church visits later, Kristen remarked to Steve that they were still searching for a new church home. They had visited several congregations and were disappointed at the lack of hospitality and the lack of follow-up response in each case. No one had personally welcomed or invited them to participate in other groups or activities of the church. The only follow-up they received came as form letters, and not all churches even did that. Kristen and Chad are an attractive, successful young adult couple with strong church backgrounds–exactly the kind of new members that most churches claim to be wanting. They are also accustomed to interacting with the public and don't radiate the "don't come near me" signal that some visitors do. Yet the initial welcomes they received and the follow-up on their visits ranged from superficial to nonexistent.

They found the greatest warmth and acceptance in a church which was considerably different than the traditions in which they had grown up. The warmth of the congregation proved more important than the differences in style of worship and local church organization.

Fred's friend Carl started attending a church in Virginia, and initially felt welcome there. He and his family became active and seemed well-accepted. When the Gulf War started, Carl found himself disagreeing strongly with the views on the war which were being expressed in worship. Carl was a pacifist and was uncomfortable with what seemed to him a pro-war sentiment that apparently was held by several in the church. He respected the right of people to disagree with him, and he expected people to respect his right to hold other views. He was disappointed.

People in the church, including the pastoral leadership, became quite angry with Carl for his peace position. Carl knew it had gone too far when church members began making threatening phone calls to his home. He felt under attack and left the congregation.

Carl and his family decided that they should seek out a congregation with a tradition as a peace church. They identified Mennonite, Brethren in Christ, and Church of the Brethren as possibilities. The warmest welcome was extended by a Church of the Brethren congregation. Within three weeks, he and his wife had made a decision–they had found a true church home. Not everyone in the church embraced the peace position of the denomination, but there was a healthy openness to differences of opinion and a hospitality that was deep rather than superficial. He later became a pastor in the denomination.

Beverley and Mike had been active in the same congregation for twenty-five years. Their daughter Shelley and her husband Bob had both grown up in that church, had been married in it, and continued to be active members. Their son Jeff moved back to the community after graduation from college. Beverley, Mike, Shelley, and Bob were more than a little shocked when Jeff explained to them that he had come to the conclusion he was gay. He didn't want to make an issue of it, but he also didn't want to hide it. Jeff's brother-in-law Bob was the first to be comfortable with the revelation of Jeff's orientation, but the others in time came to feel the same way. Beverley and Mike couldn't help wondering if they had done something which "caused" Jeff to become homosexual, but they eventually accepted his reassurances that no single factor had caused his orientation. Jeff was convinced that he didn't really decide to become a homosexual but simply recognized that he was a homosexual.

He started a job with a local company and became active in the same church the rest of his family attended. Initially people in the congregation were very enthusiastic about having him back. He was invited to join the choir and also to teach a Sunday school class, both of which were activities he greatly enjoyed.

Then word slowly began to move around the church that Jeff was gay. People began approaching Beverley, Mike, Shelley, and Bob to extend their sympathies to them, as though Jeff had a serious, incurable illness.

No one said anything directly to Jeff until the Sunday school superintendent had lunch with him. The superintendent explained that a few parents had expressed reservations about Jeff being on the teaching team for the middle school class. There was concern, the superintendent said, that perhaps Jeff would influence children in the class to become gay or that perhaps the children were not quite safe with a person who was a homosexual as their teacher. Jeff did his best to reassure the superintendent that being around a homosexual person was not going to cause someone to become homosexual and that he had no desire to influence the sexual orientation of anyone else. He said that he was offended at the implication that he might do something to harm the children.

The superintendent told Jeff that these concerns were not his own at all and apologized for appearing to be offensive. He also said he felt it best for Jeff not to continue on the teaching team. Jeff agreed, but he was heart-broken. He felt even worse when some of the children approached him, wanting to know why he had quit, and he didn't know what to say to them.

It felt to Beverley and Mike as though the pastor began making more negative references to homosexuality in his sermons than he had before Jeff's sexual orientation had become known. The pastor did not devote an entire sermon to the topic, but he was making his negative views clear. Jeff stopped attending. Beverley, Mike, Shelley, and Bob all became aware that people were acting differently around them. Mike had been the board chairperson elect, but a different person was nominated to be the new board chairperson.

Jeff emphasized to his parents and his sister that he did not want them to stop being involved in the church because of his situation. He thought that he needed to find a congregation in which he could be better accepted. Beverley, Mike, Shelley, and Bob, however, found that they themselves were no longer feeling accepted in the congregation. All of them found a new church home.

More Than a Program

The four examples just shared all reflect congregational problems in the practice of hospitality:

- Yusuf and Andrea are attempting to build a strong marriage which can support their different religious traditions. Out of respect for Andrea and genuine interest in the Christian faith, Yusuf had decided to go to both Sunday school and church with her. While those who got to know him were very affirming, he felt suspicion and, in the one instance, outright hostility from others in the congregation. It seemed to Yusuf that his very presence in the church week after week should have been confirmation that he was not like those responsible for the violence in New York and Washington.

- Kristen and Chad had difficulty finding a congregation which would display more than superficial warmth to them. They encountered the warmest hospitality in a church which was different than the traditions in which they had been raised.

- Carl and his family initially found a welcoming congregation, but the hospitality was only on the surface. When he began to express disagreement on an issue within the life of the church, he encountered not just difference of opinion but outright anger. He could have lived with the

difference of opinion, but he could not live with
threatening phone calls.

- Jeff's family had a long history with the congregation.
Clearly the issue of homosexuality is one on which people
of good faith are not always in agreement. Jeff, however,
had a kind and gentle spirit. He was not a person to be
feared. Tragically the congregation's fear of Jeff's sexual
orientation caused them not only to exclude him but to
make the rest of his family feel excluded as well.

Many factors are involved in the decision of people to choose
a church home and to remain active in congregational life.
Certainly there are theological or faith differences among
denominations which can make a difference. The peace position
of the Church of the Brethren was no doubt a better fit for Carl's
own belief system than that in the church he had been
attending.

We can't readily change the basic theological or faith
orientation of our congregations. Such changes, even when
desired by many people, take place over long periods of time.
What we can change is the willingness of people to extend a level
of warmth, of hospitality, that goes beyond the superficial and
that can embrace differences in perspective. If people leave our
churches, it should be because of genuine faith differences, not
because they have experienced rejection or felt themselves the
objects of fear.

While congregational studies, policies, and programs can
help make hospitality a reality, it is a mistake to see hospitality
as simply another program for the faith community. The practice
of hospitality, the acceptance and love of others, including
strangers, is fundamental to who we are as Christian people.
Our society teaches us to be fearful of strangers, but the New
Testament teaches a different approach:

> *Do not neglect to show hospitality to strangers,*
> *for by doing that some have entertained angels*
> *without knowing it.*
>
> Hebrews 13:2

171

As shared earlier in this book, hospitality to the stranger is assumed throughout the Old and New Testament Scriptures. Again and again, as in the Parable of the Good Samaritan, the questioning is not on the worthiness of the stranger but on the faithfulness of the one encountering the stranger. The Samaritan did not ask of the man who was injured: "Did you bring this on yourself? Why weren't you traveling with someone else for safety?" The Samaritan simply responded to the human need which was encountered. The priest and the Levite who passed by are the ones whose behavior is called into question by our Lord.

Whether we start with the assumption that the unknown person will be an enemy or a friend makes a difference! When anyone comes to our church or shows an interest in religious concerns, our starting assumption certainly should be that such a person shares with us a pull toward the heart of God. Such a person is a potential friend, perhaps sent to us by God for the enrichment of our lives. Yusuf certainly was not viewed in that way by those who made him uncomfortable, and he is very unlikely to convert to a faith tradition which made him feel under personal attack.

The work of hospitality continues long after people have become members or constituents of our congregations. We must continually be sensitive to the presence of Christ in one another, and we must be respectful of the differences of opinion and perspective which inevitably arise in any gathering of people. We should seek to be enriched by those differences rather than driven apart by them.

The Impact of Hospitality

Yusuf is unusual in his desire, as a Muslim person, to be involved in a Christian congregation. The lack of hospitality toward him, however, is indicative of a larger problem which exists in many religious communities. People like Kristen and Chad experience a lack of warmth in many churches across North America every week. There are also people who find that the churches in which they participate have inner circles which cause them to feel excluded and unwelcome. People can participate in a church for years and still feel not feel part of the congregation's social life.

In the process of studying congregational health, Christian Community has surveyed active members of churches across North America. The chart which follows summarizes the amount of agreement with three survey items in churches by category: congregations in decline; the average among all congregations; and congregations which are growing. Over fourteen hundred congregations participated in this study.

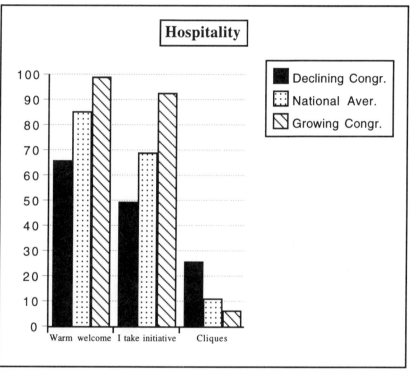

The items:

• *In our congregation, people go out of their way to extend a warm welcome to visitors and newcomers.* Almost 98% of the active members in growing congregations hold that view of their church in contrast to 66% of those in declining congregations.

• *At church, I take the initiative to talk with those I do not know well.* Responses fall some for each category on this item about personal initiative in welcoming others. The percentage is still 92% in growing congregations, but falls to 50% or below in declining congregations.

• *In our congregation, there are cliques or exclusive groups which make one feel unwelcome.* Only 6% of the active members in growing congregations have the perception that there are cliques or exclusive groups. In congregations which are in decline, the figure rises to 26% and is sometimes higher.

The same study shows that persons who have been a part of a congregation for ten years or more generally indicate that they have seven or more good friends in the congregation. That's part of the closeness which the church should make possible–the enjoyment of participating in the body of Christ. When our own needs are well met by many close friends in the church, however, it's easy to fail to reach out to others. Very few people intentionally exclude others, but the results can be very painful to some members and a complete turn-off to potential members.

The September 11, 2001 incidents also make us aware of how important it is for hospitality to be extended not just by congregations but by individuals toward those of other religions and ethnic backgrounds. While most congregations do not have the good fortune to have someone like Yusuf who wants to be a part of church life, all churches can have significant influence on attitudes toward people who are different. Congregations can help members understand the approach to faith of other religious traditions. Yet in another Christian Community study, only 8% of the participating churches had offered a class or seminar to help members better understand faiths such as Judaism, Islam, Buddhism, and Hinduism. Among those who have participated in such classes or seminars, 93% say that the experience helped them deepen their own faith; and 87% say what they learned increased their acceptance of those of other faiths.

The biblical call to hospitality has enormous implications for all of us who call ourselves Christian. Our churches need to model hospitality toward all persons, and they need to equip us to lead lives of hospitality in our homes, neighborhoods, jobs, schools, and community organizations. We need to be equipped as advocates for those who may be victims within our society.

Consider what the examples shared in this chapter, the statistical information provided, and some of the larger trends in our society suggest for our faith communities:

1. Churches which are growing have learned how to make the practice of hospitality part of the life of the entire congregation. People feel comfortable taking the initiative in reaching out to others, and visitors immediately feel a welcome that goes beyond the superficial. The life of the congregation is truly open to new people, and members expect that visitors will become friends.

Hospitality is not a program to be initiated for the purpose of church growth. We should learn about and practice hospitality because it is the right thing to do. One of the practical consequences of hospitality, however, is that churches practicing it well are usually ones which grow. Churches in which members do not show warmth to strangers are not likely to attract or retain new people.

2. People are making their church choices with less and less regard for denominational ties. This does not mean that denominational ties are without importance. Kristen and Chad first searched for a church home in the traditions with which they were most familiar. When they did not find a comfortable church home within those traditions, however, they explored other possibilities. Our churches cannot take for granted that people who grew up within the denomination will stay in the denomination.

Some people feel that we are living in a "postdenominational" time. Certainly it is true that many large Protestant denominations have experienced significant membership decline over the last two decades. That has been true for the Disciples of Christ, the Episcopal Church, the Evangelical Lutheran Church of America, the Presbyterian Church U.S.A., the United Church of Christ, the United Methodist Church, and many others.

There has also been considerable growth among some local congregations which call themselves nondenominational. Many of those congregations are relatively new, and they offer considerable energy and vitality. When a church is just starting or is growing rapidly, the hospitality of the congregation is generally very broad. New people are expected and wanted, and that is clearly communicated. People who choose these nondenominational churches are generally not so much rejecting a traditional denomination as feeling attracted to the hospitality and the energy of a newer congregation.

3. It's easy for a local church or even an entire denomination to start looking inward and to become defensive. This "circle the wagons" mentality is almost always self-defeating. We live in a time of extremely rapid social change, and many people are almost desperate for what sociologist Alvin Toffler referred to as "stability zones," places where the pace of change is much slower than in society as a whole. Many people want to see their local congregations as those stability zones. These congregations are often characterized by:

- A reluctance to accept many changes in the style of worship. There is considerable evidence that younger people respond more positively to styles of worship which are more informal and utilize drama and more contemporary music. When people want to see the church as a stability zone, they are often resistive to such changes. The more contemporary efforts are often branded as immature or "dumbing down" or "theologically superficial." What is really going on in the life of the congregation, however, usually has more to do with resistance to change than with anything about theology.

- An initial suspicion toward visitors and newer members. While new people are often given a warm initial greeting in such churches, members are in fact adopting a "wait and see" approach toward them. Will they keep coming? Are they enough like us? Will they bring change?

- An excessive concern about the physical facilities. Outreach programs for children and youth which result in possible damage to the physical facilities are quickly censored in such congregations. Church security systems are often installed to help people feel safer when the church location continues to be in a neighborhood in which relatively few of the church members live.

Rather than being people on a pilgrimage or a voyage, such congregations have become a more landed people, who feel a need to protect their turf. The church building, the continuity of the membership, and the predictability of worship and other programs become of greater importance than outreach and mission.

Criticism of such congregations, however, is not a very helpful way to bring about change. People cling to stability zones because they feel threatened, indeed fearful, in other areas of their lives. The way to help people cling less desperately to their stability zones is to help them be less fearful, more confident about the future, and better able to recognize the presence of Christ in others.

4. There is always the danger of fear driving our decision-making in the congregation as well as in our own lives and the broader society. Churches in which members feel anxious about the neighborhood and society around them are likely to put their emphasis on security systems rather than positive outreach. Many congregations have members who feel threatened by homosexuality and fail to recognize the reality that homosexuals as well as heterosexuals are God's children.

Fred has suggested to people in his seminars that many of us are spending too much time deciding what fish we want to catch rather than just putting out the net and taking the fish we reach. Many of us have become too concerned about excluding certain types of people and making value judgments. This applies not only to our attitude toward homosexual people but also to our attitude toward persons who have drug and alcohol problems or who are single parents. The statistical information shared opposite the first page of this chapter notes large differences in attitudes toward people who have problems with addictions and toward single parents between churches which are growing and churches which are in decline. People in churches which are growing are far more likely to feel that people from such backgrounds can find welcome and acceptance.

When we truly learn to recognize Christ in others, then diversity does not represent a threat to us. Seeing Christ in others enables us to open ourselves to the blessings we can receive from those who are different and enables us to be the channels through which God can share blessings with others.

5. When hospitality is superficial rather than deep, we may gain new members, but we will not successfully integrate them into congregational life. Visitors are often attracted to long established churches because they sense that there are stability zones and relationships that matter. They observe people caring about one another and a large number of social groupings that may be more informal than part of the church's official program. This can be especially true in churches which have many members who are connected by family ties. Visitors want to be part of that kind of community.

In *A Christian View of Hospitality–Expecting Surprises*, Michele Hershberger shares this perspective on what often happens to new people who are attracted to such churches:

> *We are friendly to them and seek to include them as much as we can. But the very thing that attracts them also puts them outside the circle. The very thing that they want so much to be a part of, they can't be a part of completely, no matter how hard they try, because they don't have the same last names. They don't catch the inside jokes* [p. 187].

The key to change, of course, is to have a hospitality which moves beyond the superficial, which enables us to recognize the presence of Christ in others. That perspective brings enthusiasm for new people and a willingness to integrate them into the social life of the congregation as well as into worship and programs.

6. Our churches, at their best, should be forces for peace and justice within the broader society. Politicians and the news media may promote fear, but the church should not be part of that process. Those of us who belong to the church should be alert for opportunities to help people be more at peace with one another and less driven by fear in the decisions that they make. We should be concerned about how our government agencies and social service institutions treat those charged with crimes and those victimized by crimes. We should be concerned about juveniles who are in trouble with drugs, the law, or both. We should be advocates for those of other religious traditions and ethnic backgrounds.

Our congregations should be places where people can talk about difficult topics that are avoided elsewhere. Our churches should be places where:

- Problems between blacks and whites and those involving other races can be openly and honestly discussed. Our churches should be seeking ways to connect people of different races, whether they belong to the same church or not.

- Young people can feel comfortable talking about sexual decision-making, dating, and marriage. If we are truly concerned about the moral development of youth, then the church should be a moral leader and a safe place for young people to receive the information they need to make intelligent decisions in these important areas.

- Problems in our schools and educational concerns can be discussed. Our churches generally have both parents and educators involved and have the potential to offer a forum not as controlled by political agenda and posturing as happens in the broader community. Juvenile crime and related issues also need to be discussed in our church settings.

- Opportunities are provided to learn about those of other faith traditions and cultures. Rather than being threatened by differences, we should have confidence that learning about other faiths is likely to deepen our own beliefs. A peaceful world rests on a foundation of true understanding and respect among persons who are different.

Sometimes our congregations decide to become active forces for peace and justice in the community by an institutional presence or involvement. At other times, our congregations may be the settings which equip us individually to be forces for peace and justice in the broader society.

Let Us Know

We would like to know what experiences you have in living out a deeper hospitality as an individual and as part of a faith community. If you have an experience you'd like to share, write to us at:

Fred Bernhard and Steve Clapp
LifeQuest
6404 S. Calhoun Street
Fort Wayne, Indiana 46807

DadofTia@aol.com

Study Guide

This *Study Guide* is designed for use by individuals and groups wanting to think more deeply about the issues raised in **Hospitality: Life in a Time of Fear**. While a few community-based groups may decide to share in this study, most groups will likely be church-based: Sunday school classes, Bible study groups, church boards, membership committees, and mission groups.

Individuals using this *Study Guide* may want to record their responses to questions in a spiral-bound notebook or journal. Some of the activities are clearly more appropriate for use by groups than by individuals. Ten of the sessions relate to specific sections of the book (the *Introduction* plus nine chapters); three delve further into issues raised by the book. Here are a few suggestions if you are doing this study with a class or group:

- Remember that every group has both active and passive learners. Encourage, but do not force, participation. Allow "I pass" as an acceptable response.
- Having class members use different translations of the Bible will enrich your discussion and give new perspective.
- Sessions assume that a chalkboard or newsprint is available.
- While your sessions will be smoother if group members read the chapters in advance, it's not generally wise to assume that all have done so! Provide summaries to help those who have not read the material and to refresh those who have.
- We recommend that you open and close sessions with prayer.

Session One
Introduction to *Hospitality: Life in a Time of Fear*, pages 7-21

1. What were you doing when you learned of the events of September 11, 2001? How do your experiences of that day compare with those of Steve and Fred as shared on pages 7-8? How closely connected are you to persons who were killed or injured that day? How closely connected are you to someone else who knows persons who were killed or injured?

2. Pages 9-12 contain several examples of persons affected by the events of September 11, 2001, or by anxiety over possible future terrorist activity. With which persons do you most strongly identify? Why? In what ways, if any, do you think you own life is different since the events of that day?

3. Think about the most recent newscast you heard on the radio or saw on television. In what ways does the newscast reflect our time being the Information Age? In what ways does the newscast reinforce the concept of our time as an Age of Fear (see page 13)? Or look at today's newspaper, and consider the same questions.

4. Contrast the message of **Ecclesiastes 3:1-8** with that of **Matthew 7:24-27** (see pages 16-17). How many of the seasons described in Ecclesiastes have you experienced in your own life? Which of those

verses best describe your life as you experience it today? In what ways do the events of September 11, 2001 make us more aware of the importance of a firm foundation for our lives? Do you agree or disagree with the three things we can count on which are discussed on pages 17-19? Why?

5. Page 20 asserts that "blessings flow to us as we recognize the presence of Christ in others and reach out to one another." In what persons do you most easily see the presence of Christ? In what persons do you find it most difficult to recognize Christ's presence?

Session Two
Chapter One in *Hospitality: Life in a Time of Fear*, pages 23-33

1. "What do you fear?" Make a list of the things that you fear (on chalkboard or newsprint if doing this as a group). Go through the list:
   - Mark with an "H" each fear that seems to you healthy.
   - Mark with a "UH" each fear that seems to you unhealthy.
   - Mark with a "?" each fear that could be healthy or unhealthy depending on the circumstances.
   - Mark with a "M" each fear that is a MAJOR one to you.
   - Mark with an "L" each fear that you think is LIKELY to happen.

If doing this as a class or group, invite everyone to contribute to the list of fears. Then do hand counts to see how many feel that each fear is healthy, unhealthy, . . . Talk about the responses.

2. Look at the list of categories (pages 25-26) which play on our fears (politicians, television dramas, and motion pictures, . . .). What personal experiences have you had of fears being caused or reinforced by those sources? What other persons or forces in society play on our fears?

3. Read **Psalm 111**, noting especially verse 10: "The fear of the LORD is the beginning of wisdom; all those who practice it have a good understanding." Many people think the word *fear* in this context means obedience or love or commitment. Why is this kind of fear important? Should a person who is knowingly disobedient fear God? Why, or why not?

4. Reflect on the section titled "We Are Changed" which begins on page 26. Also note the "Tips from the United States Postal Service" found on page 22. How do you think the country as a whole has been changed? How have your friends and coworkers been changed? How have you been changed as an individual? What impact has the threat of terrorism had on your family?

5. Pages 32-33 talk about the importance of developing a healthy spiritual life, specially as expressed in Philippians 3:13b-14 and

Romans 8:38-39. How would you assess the current status of your spiritual life? To what extent do the events of the past hold you back from a healthy spiritual life? To what extent have events of the past nurtured your spiritual life?

Session Three
Chapter Two in *Hospitality: Life in a time of Fear*, pages 35-51

1. Look at "Anthrax and Other Biological Weapons" on page 34. In what ways are germs "the poor man's atom bomb"? How much fear do you have of bioterrorism? Why is this danger such a great source of anxiety to many people?

2. Do the "What Do We Fear?" exercise on pages 39-43. If you are in a group, talk about your responses with others (ideally in groups of three or four people). How do the fears identified in this list compare with those you identified yourself in the last session?

3. What factors in our society contribute to loneliness? In what ways do e-mail and the Internet contribute to loneliness? In what ways do e-mail and the Internet help people better connect with others? Note the example on pages 46-47 of the 82-year-old woman not yet adjusted after the death of her husband. How do people best deal with the loneliness or emptiness that comes with the loss of a parent, a spouse, or a child? Why are the losses people experienced on September 11, 2001, so difficult for us as individuals and a society?

4. Reflect on **Hebrews 13:2**–"Do not neglect to show hospitality to strangers, for by doing that some have entertained angels without knowing it." Then look at the definitions of hospitality on pages 49 and 50. Are these definition consistent with the message of Hebrews 13:2? Why, or why not? How does this way of viewing strangers differ from the way of secular society?

5. Do you know anyone who has had an experience like Mable's (as described at the start of the chapter)? If you are in a group, share such experiences with others. What might have prevented that experience for Mable? Is there any way to be completely safe? Why, or why not? What price do we pay when we are too driven by our fears? How does a person build confidence after an experience like Mable's?

Session Four
Chapter Three in *Hospitality: Life in a time of Fear*, pages 53-69

1. What experiences have you or people you know had with extreme sports like mountain climbing, sky diving, bungee jumping, or BASE jumping? Note some of Melanie's observations about the attraction of

mountain climbing. What do you think are the reasons for the popularity of extreme sports? How can these activities produce spiritual experiences? Do such activities help people overcome fears? Why, or why not?

2. Note this quote from page 55: "Many of us, however, do not seek to develop the spiritual life with the same energy that we put into gaining an education, earning a living, participating in sports, or even keeping the house clean. Thus the spiritual life becomes one part of who we are, but not the center of our being." How do you feel about that statement? If you are in a group, use masking tape to put a line on the floor that is numbered from **1** to **10**. Make the line long enough that people can stand along it. Let **1** represent a very low amount of effort, and let **10** represent a very high amount of effort. Ask people to stand along the line to show the amount of effort which they typically expend on:
- Job or career
- Home upkeep and improvement
- Sports (observing or participating)
- Physical fitness
- The spiritual life

Provide opportunity to talk about responses as people stand in place before moving to the next item on the list. How have the events of September 11, 2001, caused many of us to think more seriously about the spiritual life?

3. Note the biblical verses on the fear of God which are on pages 57-58. With which Scriptures do you most strongly identify? Why? Then read **1 John 4:16-20** which talks about perfect love casting out fear. How do you reconcile what 1 John says with some of the other biblical verses quoted on fear? Is the meaning of fear different in some of these quotations? If so, in what ways?

4. Pages 59-61 talk about the hospitality shown by Abraham and Sarah. How would we change our hospitality toward strangers today if we took those words seriously? Read **Matthew 25:31-46,** which talks about discovering Christ in other people, particularly in the hungry, the naked, the imprisoned. Do we really believe those words in our society? Why, or why not? Reflect on this statement from page 62: "Our relationships with others are transformed when we seriously consider the reality that we are encountering Christ in the other person. That should affect all of our relationships, every day of our lives." Do these words suggest that Christ is present even in those who do not believe in him? Why, or why not? How would the belief that Christ is present in everyone affect our view of those we are inclined to dislike? Of those with differing values and beliefs? Of those with differing lifestyles?

5. Review the material on handguns and gun violence on pages 64-67. If you are with a group, be sensitive to the fact that there may be strong, differing opinions on these issues. Why are weapons an appropriate spiritual concern? Why have guns become such an important part of society in the United States? What role do television and motion pictures play in the desire of people to own guns? Why does fear have so much to do with gun ownership?

Session Five
Chapter Four in *Hospitality: Life in a Time of Fear*, pages 71-87

1. If you are meeting as a group, bring a cat or dog to share in your time together. Reflect on the efforts of Roberto (see page 71) to use pets as a way to build relationships. Why do so many people respond warmly to pets? Is it easier to show hospitality to pets than to people? Why, or why not? Invite people to share stories of ways that pets have positively linked them to other people.

2. Reflect on the section "Bad Things Do Happen, But. . ." which begins on page 74. What are the roots of some of these fears in our society? Who gains because of these fears? How can a person exercise reasonable caution without being overwhelmed by fear?

3. Read **Ephesians 6:10-17**, noting especially verse 12, which is quoted on page 78. What are the "cosmic powers" at work in our world? How do we cope with forces of evil in our time? Why is it important to be alert to feelings of hate as a warning sign for the spiritual life? How can God protect us against the cosmic powers?

4. Reflect on the story of Margaret (pages 79-82), who lost her son and her husband. Do you think Margaret actually came to feel that homosexuality was "all right"? Why, or why not? Is it necessary to approve of someone else's lifestyle in order to love that person? Why, or why not? Why are some people in our society so frightened of homosexual persons? How can the church help us with our fears?

5. Complete "A Quiz on the Islamic Faith" on page 85, and compare your responses with those on pages 86-87. What, if anything, did you learn from the quiz and responses? Why do so many of us in North America know relatively little about the Islamic faith? How does lack of knowledge make it more difficult for us to relate to Muslim people?

6. Look at the examples of transformed lives on pages 82-84. With which of those do you most strongly identify? What similar examples of transformation have you experienced or observed? What gifts do we receive from strangers?

Session Six

Chapter Five in *Hospitality: Life in a Time of Fear*, pages 89-105

1. Think about times in your own life when you have experienced answered prayer or about experiences with prayer that others have shared with you. If you are in a group, share those with one another. When do people most commonly pray? Why do people pray? Are there particular settings or circumstances, other than church, which cause people to be more likely to pray? Why? Will the habits of more frequent prayer begun by some people on September 11, 2001, continue into the future?

2. Reflect on the stories about the cockatiel and about Hillary and Brad (89-92). What instances of problems in showing hospitality have you experienced? Do you think Steve and Sara have any regrets about the effort spent helping the cockatiel? Why or why not? Do you think Hillary and Brad have regrets? Why, or why not? Why is it important to help people even when there are risks involved?

3. How do you feel about the Roman Catholic young adult who has stopped flying because he has dark skin and a Middle Eastern sounding name (page 93)? Would you feel differently if he were Muslim? How would you feel about life in North America if you were a Muslim? What role does prayer play in how we relate to others?

4. Look at the guidelines for prayer on pages 96-99. What additional guidelines would you add to this list? Which of the guidelines is most difficult for you to implement in your own life?

5. Read about prayers of rejoicing in **Philippians 4:4-7**. How do prayers of thanksgiving or rejoicing help us? How do prayers for God's guidance and strength help us? Why is it important to pray for God's forgiveness? It has been said that "it is dangerous to ask God for something, because he may give it to you." What does that statement mean to you? Do you agree or disagree with it? Why?

6. Spend time in prayer. If you are part of a group, assign some of the prayers on pages 100-105 to group members to be prayed aloud. OR share your own prayers.

Session Seven

Chapter Six in *Hospitality: Life in a Time of Fear*, pages 107-123

1. Prepare as many notecards as there are members of your group. On each card, write one of the following:
   - A good family moment or experience.
   - An awkward or painful family moment or experience.
   - A funny family moment or experience.

186

- A memorable family moment or experience.
- An example of forgiveness within a family.
- A positive family connection between grandparents and grandchildren.

Put them in a small box or hat, and have each person draw one. Then invite people to share something based on the card drawn. Explain that these do not have to be experiences in your own family–they can be any family experience you've observed or of which you've heard. If people do not want to share, it's fine of course to say "I PASS." If your group is large, you may want to do this sharing in smaller groups of three to five persons.

2. Reflect on the experiences of Carolyn and her daughter Jill and of Keith and his wife Becky (pages 107-109). What similar experiences have you had or observed? In what ways does hospitality, seeing other family members as guests and the children of God, relate to these experiences?

3. Consider the material on children which begins on page 109. Which of the implications for parenting seem to you the most important? Thinking about parenting from the perspective of hospitality, what additional perspectives or guidelines would you suggest? The book quotes a psychologist: "The problem for most of us is that we don't do enough to influence the behavior of our children when they are small and then that we try to regain control when they become teenagers." Do you agree with that view? Why, or why not? What new concerns for parenting are raised by the events of September 11, 2001, and by concern about terrorism.

4. Consider the material on spouses and significant others which begins on page 115. The authors talk about the problem of spouses and significant others receiving our leftovers of time, energy, patience, and caring. Why does this happen so frequently? What can be done to prevent this? Why are control issues so difficult in a marriage or in a committed relationship?

5. Study **Isaiah 25:6** on the power of sharing food together and **Luke 14:13-14** on broad invitations to the banquet. What are the implications of these passages for your life? How do these passages relate to the centrality of the dining room table in Steve's home (pages 119-121)? What object or area of your home has or could have a significance similar to that of the table in his childhood home?

Session Eight
Chapter Seven in *Hospitality: Life in a Time of Fear*, pages 125-149

1. Share with others examples of rudeness you've experienced in restaurants, grocery stores, traffic, work settings, churches, your

neighborhood, airports, hospitals, and/or schools. Why has rude-ness become so commonplace in our society? How can hospitality make a difference?

2. If you are doing this study as part of a group, invite individuals or smaller groups to focus on a particular section of this chapter:
• Behind the Wheel
• At the Airport
• In the Neighborhood
• The Workplace
• Dealing with Telephone Solicitations
• E-mail and the Internet
• Business and Community Contacts
• Wherever Possible

Have each person or smaller group identify what seems most important from the assigned section and also brainstorm any additional ideas for showing greater hospitality in that area of life. Have observations shared with the whole group.

3. Page 147 reminds us that: "Simple resolutions to be 'friendlier' won't result in deep change in our habits or in the attitudes of others." Read again **Hebrews 13:2**. Why is it so important to recognize the presence of angels or of Christ in others? Why is it so difficult for us to do this on a daily basis? How can prayer aid in the deepening of the spiritual life and in the practice of hospitality?

4. Reflect on the bulleted items on page 148 which raise additional strategies or possibilities for sharing hospitality. Which of those would work well in your life? What additional possibilities can you identify?

5. In the discussion of faith-sharing, page 149 asserts: "We do not have to manipulate in order for those opportunities to come; God will bring them to us if we are open to receiving them." Do you agree with that statement? Why, or why not? Is that statement reassuring, frightening, or both?

Session Nine
Chapter Eight in *Hospitality: Life in a Time of Fear*, pages 151-161

1. Reflect on the experiences of Frank McCourt which are shared in the beginning of this chapter. Contrast his experiences with our relative isolation today from persons with extreme physical needs. Do you have a person who is very poor as one of your four or five closest friends? Do you have a person who is very rich as one of your four or five closest friends? Do you have a person of a different ethnic background as one of your four or five closest friends? What about a person of a non-Christian religion? What do we miss by not having

greater diversity in our lives? How does the lack of diversity in our lives contribute to fearfulness in our society?

2. Reflect on the material about crime, perhaps assigning each of these topics to an individual or a smaller group:
- Juvenile Crime
- Problems in Jails and Prisons
- Severe Sentences

Invite each individual or smaller group to share observations about the assigned topic. Why is it so difficult to make changes in our criminal justice system? What is it appropriate to have some fear of crime? How do those fears immobilize us and cause harm? What changes are realistic?

3. Read **Jeremiah 17:9** on evil and the human heart, and look at the quote from Solzhenitsyn on page 158. Why is it more comfortable to think about there being a group of people in society who are clearly evil than to consider the possibility of evil residing in each of our hearts? Page 157 raises this concern: "We have in fact not thought about the persons who commit crimes as being our brothers and sisters in Christ." What difference would that perspective make?

4. Consider the five suggestions on response to crime which are found on pages 158-159. Which of those suggestions do you think are most important? Which are most realistic? What additional suggestions would you make? What personal experiences have you had which relate to these suggestions?

5. Look at the list of things people can do found on pages 160-161. What would you add to this list? What, if anything, should churches be doing in these areas? What would you like to do as an individual?

Session Ten
Chapter Nine in *Hospitality: Life in a Time of Fear*, pages 162-180

1. You are reading these words a few months or a few years after the events of September 11, 2001. To what extent are churches and individual Christians still showing the kinds of responses shared on pages 163-164? How many of the suggestions on pages 164-166 have been utilized in your congregation? Are there other actions you would like to see taken by your church and its leaders?

2. Reflect on the experiences of Yusuf and Andrea (with Yusuf a Muslim person), Kristen and Chad (searching for a new church home), Carl (concerned about peace issues), and Jeff (who had a homosexual orientation). What kind of welcome would they experience in your congregation? How would you personally relate to them?

3. What kinds of people do you find it easiest to show hospitality? Most difficult? Page 173 says: "We should seek to be enriched by those differences rather than driven apart by them." Why are those words easier to say than to put into practice? What categories of persons from your community are absent from your church? What does **Genesis 18:1-15** suggest about hospitality to all people?

4. Consider the chart on page 174 which makes comparisons between growing and declining congregations. How would people in your church respond to the three items shown on the chart? What improvements are needed in your church?

5. Pages 175-180 include six statements or perspectives. Which are most relevant for your congregation? Why is it crucial for hospitality to be more than just another church program? How can church programs help make hospitality a reality?

Optional Session Eleven–A Visitors Perspective: If you are studying this book as part of a church class or group, gain the perspective of visitors and/or recent members. Invite a couple of people who have visited your church in the past year and a couple of people who have recently joined your church to meet with your group. Share Chapter Nine with them in advance of their meeting with your group. Invite them to share what it was like to visit your congregation. What improvements could be made? What did they appreciate about the warmth of their reception? How do new members feel about the way they have been able to become involved in the programs and the social life of the congregation?

Optional Session Twelve–Outside Perspective: Have a guest speaker for this session who can share some insights into a category of persons with whom people in our society are often uncomfortable. Possibilities would include: a prison chaplain, a person who has been in prison, a person from a social service or religious organization who deals with racial tensions and can speak frankly about race relations in your community, a person of homosexual orientation who is comfortable talking about the problems faced by people of that orientation, or a member of the Muslim faith. Provide a copy of *Hospitality: Life in a Time of Fear* to the guest speaker in advance of your meeting, so that person can become familiar with what you have been studying. If you are reflecting on this material as an individual rather than as part of a group, consider inviting a person in one of the above categories to share a meal with you.

Optional Session Thirteen–Overview: Spend a final session thinking about what has been learned during the course of this study. What issues remain unresolved for you? What further study would you like to do in the area of hospitality?

Resources

An asterisk (*) indicates books available from LifeQuest (page 192).

Armstrong, Karen, *Islam: A Short History* (Modern Library), 2000. An excellent history of the Islamic faith which helps one understand how Muslim people have been affected by the Western world.

*Bernhard, Fred and Steve Clapp, *Widening the Welcome of Your Church* (LifeQuest), 1996, 1997, 1999, 2000. A very practical book which shows how biblical hospitality can revitalize a congregation. For individual reading or group study.

*Clapp, Steve, *Overcoming Barriers to Church Growth* (The Andrew Center and LifeQuest), 1994. For people who have difficulty getting the congregation interested in outreach. Includes a very helpful section on low self-esteem in individuals, congregations, and denominations as a sometimes overlooked barrier.

*Detwiler, Sam and Steve Clapp, *Sharing Living Water* (LifeQuest), 1996, 2000, 2001. How to share the faith in comfortable, nonmanipulative ways. For individual reading or group study.

Foster, Richard J., *Prayer–Finding the Heart's True Home* (HarperSanFrancisco), 1992. A truly wonderful book about prayer and the ways in which prayer can move us to personal transformation, greater intimacy with God, and more meaningful ministry to others.

Fox, Matthew, *Confessions* (HarperSanFrancisco), 1996. Emphasizes a broader acceptance of all people and a recognition of God's presence in the natural world.

Glassner, Barry, *The Culture of Fear* (Basic Books), 1999. An outstanding book that examines the role of irrational fear in contemporary culture and explores some of the causes of that fear.

Hasan, Asma Gull, *American Muslims: The New Generation* (Continuum), 2000. Tremendously helpful in understanding the Islamic faith and Muslim people from the perspective of a young Muslim woman who was raised in the United States.

*Hershey, S. Joan, *The First Thirty Seconds: A Guide to Hospitality for Greeters and Ushers* (LifeQuest), 2000. Gives practical strategies to help church greeters and ushers, who are on the front lines of hospitality, create a warm experience for all who come.

Hershberger, Michele, *A Christian View of Hospitality–Expecting Surprises* (Herald Press), 1999. An excellent overview of hospitality–primarily from a congregational point of view.

Kelly, Thomas R., *A Testament of Devotion* (HarperSanFrancisco), 1941, 1942. Profound implications for the development of the inner life and for the quality of our relationships with others.

McCourt, Frank, *Angela's Ashes* (Scribner), 1996. Describes extremely harsh living conditions, the practice of kindness in the midst of great poverty, and the inner strength that pulled Frank McCourt through those days.

Mendel, Richard, *Less Hype, More Help–Reducing Juvenile Crime*. Available online at www.aypf.org or can be obtained from the American Youth Policy Forum, 1836 Jefferson Place, NW, Washington, DC 20036 for $5.00 to cover postage and handling (prepaid orders only, please).

Miller, Judith, Stephen Engelberg, and William Broad, *Germs: Biological Weapons and America's Secret War* (Simon & Schuster), 2001. A balanced, insightful look at the threat of bioterrorism.

Nouwen, Henri J.M., *Reaching Out* (Doubleday), 1975. An absolutely wonderful book dealing with the spiritual basis for hospitality.

Rivers, Caryl, *Slick Spins and Fractured Facts* (Columbia University Press), 1996. An intelligent and helpful look at how news media in particular shape our view of the world in sometimes unhealthy ways.

Wright, Wendy M., *Sacred Dwelling: A Spirituality of Family Life* (Forest of Peace Publishing, Leavenworth, Kansas), 1994. A very helpful book on the development of spirituality in the home.
****
Web Sites of Interest:
www.cmcu.net – Georgetown University's Center for Muslim-Christian Understanding.
www.firstgov.gov/featured/usgresponse.html – Official government site with information on victims assistance, bioterrorism, mental health assistance, and more. Helpful links.
islam.about.com/cs/women – Information on Muslim women.
www.islam-online.net/english/discover/discover.shtml – Islam.
www.usccr.gov/tragedy/main.htm – U.S. Commission on Civil Rights.
www.people-press.org/terrep.htm – Pew Research Center on terrorism.
www.gallup.com/poll/releases – Gallup Poll information.
www.ces.purdue.edu/terrorism/children – Purdue University Extension on Terrorism and Children.
****
For information about quantity orders of this publication or about our other resources, contact:
LifeQuest
6404 S. Calhoun Street • Fort Wayne, IN 46807 • U.S.A.
219-744-6510 (General Inquiries) • 419-872-7448 (Orders)
DadofTia@aol.com • www.churchstuff.com (Renovation Underway)